INSTANT POT COOKBOOK For Beginners 550

Easy & Most Foolproof Instant Pot Recipes Cookbook for Everyday Cooking

BY

Francis Michael

ISBN: 978-1-952504-37-2

COPYRIGHT © 2020 by Francis Michael

All rights reserved. This book is copyright protected and it's for personal use only. Without the prior written permission of the publisher, no part of this publication should be reproduced, distributed, or transmitted in any form or by any means, including photocopying, recording, or other electronic or mechanical methods.

This book is sold with the idea that the author is not needed to render accounting, officially permitted, or otherwise, qualified services. It's recommended to seek for the services of a legal or professional, a practiced individual in the profession if advice is needed.

DISCLAIMER

The information written in this publication is geared for educational and entertainment purposes only. Concerted efforts have been made towards providing accurate, up to date and reliable complete information. The information in this book is true and complete to the best of our knowledge.

Neither the publisher nor the author takes any responsibility for any possible consequences of reading or enjoying the recipes in this book. The author and publisher disclaim any liability in connection with the use of information contained in this book. Under no circumstance will any legal responsibility or blame be apportioned against the author or publisher for any reparation, damages, or monetary loss due to the information herein, either directly or indirectly.

Table of Contents

INTRODUCTION ... 7
- What is an Instant Pot? ... 7
- Reasons Why You Need An Instant Pot ... 8
- Making Sense Of Those Buttons ... 10
- Step-By-Step Guide to Clean Your Instant Pot ... 13

INSTANT POT BREAKFAST RECIPES ... 15
- Breakfast Cobbler ... 15
- Pumpkin Spice Latte Oats ... 16
- Crustless Tomato Spinach Quiche ... 17
- Berries and Cream Breakfast Cake ... 18
- Mushroom Risotto ... 20
- Hidden Cauliflower Mac 'n' Cheese ... 21
- Breakfast Burritos ... 22
- Vanilla Latte Steel Cut Oats ... 23
- Macaroni and Cheese ... 24
- Buckwheat Porridge ... 25
- Caldo Verde ... 26
- Brown Butter Steel-Cut Oatmeal ... 27

INSTANT POT SOUP & STEW RECIPES ... 28
- Vietnamese Chicken Noodle Soup ... 28
- Italian Beef Stew ... 30
- Vegetable Soup ... 31
- Italian Sausage Stew ... 32
- Cheddar Broccoli & Potato Soup ... 34
- Ham Gnocchi Soup ... 35
- Spanish Infused Chicken Stew ... 36
- Chicken Noodle Soup ... 37
- Tomato Chick Pea Soup ... 38
- Creamy Thai Coconut Chicken Soup ... 39
- Smoky Lentil and Potato Soup ... 40

INSTANT POT FISH & SEAFOOD RECIPES ... 41
- Shrimp Scampi ... 41
- Steamed Alaskan Crab Legs ... 42

10-Minute Instant Pot Salmon 43

Shrimp Paella 44

Coconut Fish Curry 45

Chipotle Shrimp Soup 47

Cajun Shrimp and Sausage Boil 48

Lemon Pepper Salmon 50

Lobster Bisque 51

Cioppino Seafood Stew 52

INSTANT POT POULTRY RECIPES 54

Teriyaki Chicken and Rice 54

Salsa Lime Chicken 55

Chicken Adobo 56

Turkey Breast 57

Honey Garlic Chicken 58

Mongolian Chicken 59

Creamy Italian Chicken Breasts 61

Chicken Marsala 62

Chicken Cordon Bleu 63

Chicken Chile Verde 64

INSTANT POT BEAN & GRAIN RECIPES 65

Refried Black Beans 65

Spiced Coconut Chicken and Rice 66

Mexican Rice and Beans 68

New Orleans-Style Red Beans and Rice 69

Pinto Beans & Ham Hocks 70

Chicken Tinga & Black Bean Tacos 71

Mexican Pinto Beans 73

Cherry & Spice Rice Pudding 74

INSTANT POT LAMB, BEEF & PORK RECIPES 75

Beef and Butternut Squash Stew 75

Boneless Pork Chops 77

Sticky Hoisin Baby Back Ribs 78

Japanese Pork Tender Rib Stew 79

Cuban Pulled Pork Sandwiches 81

- Pork Vindaloo 83
- Korean Beef 84
- Pork Chops 85
- Lamb Stew 86
- Hearty Beef Stew 87

INSTANT POT EGG RECIPES 88
- Poached Eggs 88
- Bacon Cheddar Egg Casserole 89
- Eggy Muffins 90
- Sous Vide Egg Bites 91
- Sriracha and Red Pepper Deviled Eggs 92
- Egg Pudding 93
- Cheesy Egg Bake 94
- Chinese Savory Steamed Egg 95
- Hard Boiled Eggs 96
- Quick Egg Custard 97
- French "Baked" Eggs 98
- Artichoke and Asparagus Deviled Eggs 99

INSTANT POT VEGAN & VEGETARIAN RECIPES 100
- Vegan Cauliflower Queso 100
- Veggie Chickpea Potato Soup 102
- Potato Corn Chowder 104
- Mushroom Bourguignon 105
- Vegan Potato Curry 106
- Vegan Lentil Chili 107
- Maple Bourbon Sweet Potato Chili 108
- Green Chile Stew 110
- Vegetable Barley Soup 112
- Vegan Butter Chicken 113

INSTANT POT APPETIZER RECIPES 115
- Homemade Peaches and Cream Oatmeal 115
- Cocktail Meatballs 116
- Buffalo Ranch Chicken Dip 117
- Beer-Braised Pulled Ham 118

- Cranberry Pecan Brie 119
- Prosciutto-wrapped Asparagus Canes 120
- Barbecue Kielbasa Bites 121
- Apple Pie Steel Cut Oats 122
- Cheddar Bacon Ale Dip 123
- Hoisin Meatballs 124

INSTANT POT DESSERT RECIPES 125
- Blueberry Cornmeal Breakfast Cake 125
- Apple Bread with Salted Caramel Icing 126
- Chunky Apple Cake 127
- Apple Crisp 128
- Molten Mocha Cake 129
- Mason Jar Steel Cut Oats 130
- Applesauce 131

INTRODUCTION

What is an Instant Pot?

The Instant Pot is an electronic cooking device or machine programmed to perform the function of 7 gadgets. Unlike electric pressure cooker, steamer, slow cooker, yoghurt maker, rice cooker, warming pot or sauté pan, Instant Pot is a cooker programmed with multi-functions which can perform the same task like the afore mentioned machines. The Instant Pot is a seven-in-one multi cooker combined that can work as an electric pressure cooker, steamer, slow cooker, yoghurt maker, rice cooker, and sauté pan. It can cook meals instantly and faster but it has an option for a start time that can be programmed to delay.

Some people that likes convenient cooking and the option of "set it and forget it" in a slow cooker would have a great passion for Instant Pot and also including those who desires to have a pressure cooker, steamer, yoghurt maker and slow cooker simultaneously but has little or no space to occupy the four cookers, Instant Pot performs the same functions like the other four machines. The Instant Pot comes with instruction manual and short booklet of recipes which contain functions of Instant Pot and manufacturer's recommended quantities of food ingredients together with preparation and cooking times to help the newbies.

The Instant Pot will save you a whole lots of time if you wants to cook food like stew, lentils or grains. The special thing about Instant Pot is that it has a lot of functional uses for a single appliance and you can set it and walk away doing other things while the machine does its magic. With its multi-functional ability, it may seem difficult to operate your Instant Pot but it's very easy to operate when you follow the instruction manual.

Reasons Why You Need An Instant Pot

1. It Can Cook Beans Super-Fast:

This reason alone got my attention to this fabulous Instant Pot device. While it takes some people about 12-15 minutes to cook soaked beans and 37-40 minutes to cook dry beans. I was not fully convinced when the Instant Pot cook beans very fast until I heard it over and over again from different people and their good comments made about their Instant Pot. That was when I started having great passion for Instant Pot and it earned a space in my kitchen.

2. To Make Perfect Brown Rice:

It's not easy to cook brown rice but it was easy for me. I have been thinking brown rice was easy to cook but was doubtful the first time I cooked brown rice with little water and I thought I would made crunchy rice. However, the rice was not crunchy as I thought and it was perfect rice I have ever cooked. You can use your Instant Pot to make recipes like Mexican Casserole, Cheesy Broccoli and Rice Casserole perfectly in a fraction of the time.

3. Steam/Cook Veggies in Minutes:

The Instant Pot cooks veggies in minutes. When cooking veggies, do not walk away to avoid burning or overcooking your veggies. It's important to stick to the step by step recipes instructions when cooking veggies. I've burned more than my fair share of veggies by forgetting about them. You have to make use of quick pressure release to release the steam once they are finished cooking.

4. Built in Timer:

What amazes me the most about the Instant Pot machine is the fact that you can cook a meal, walk away and come back later to meet fully cooked meals. The Instant Pot will not start cooking by itself until you want it to cook by using the timer. You can program your dinner to start at 4:30pm and keep it warm until you get home.

5. Easy Clean Up:

Washing of my dishes is one of the things I have little time to do. I do avoid cooking dishes that will require thorough washing of dishes. When it comes to Instant Pot, it is very easy to clean up after use.

6. Pressure Cooking Retains More Nutrients:

Researchers have it that food cooked for a short time with less water retains more nutrients. Instant Pot retains more nutrients because of its short duration used for cooking. Due to the high pressure, beans and grains become more digestible.

7. They are Safe:

There are some reports on injuries or dangers of pressure cookers blowing up while cooking. Some people became scared of using pressure cooker because of some domestic violence caused by the pressure cooker. However, Instant Pot is very safe to use. It has 10 in-built safety features which include high temperature warning, a lid which is to be locked while cooking, automatic pressure control and many others.

8. Slow Cooker:

The Instant Pot is a little taller but has the same size with slow cookers. The Instant Pot also perform the function of a slow cooker by just pressing a button. Some people may decide to use their Instant Pot as a slow cooker on regular bases. By doing this, you must make sure you buy the optional lid so you can be able to use the Instant Pot as a slow cooker on regular basis.

9. Sauté feature:

The Instant Pot has a sauté feature. It means the Instant Pot can also perform the function of a sauté pan. So you can toss onions and garlic in, select sauté button, prepare the rest of your ingredients and then add them to the pot and set the time you want Instant Pot to cook whatever you wants to cook.

Making Sense Of Those Buttons

1. **Manual / Pressure Buttons:**

    This function will be frequently used which enables you to select the cooking time manually and pressure cook what you wants to cook. The Instant Pot pressure, time and temperature can be adjusted by pressing the "+/-" features. It is imperative to follow the recipe instructions to know if you are to pressure cook the food using Low or High Pressure. The "Manual" and "Pressure" button stands for pressure cooking unlike functions like "Sauté", "Yogurt" or "Slow cooker" which does not require pressure cooking. The Instant Pot's default setting is High Pressure when you press the "Manual" button.

2. **Sauté Button:**

    This feature is the second most frequently used button on the Instant Pot. You can select the sauté button to cook up anything as you would in a skillet or pan without 1 cup of liquid. All you need to do is just to set the "Sauté" button, add some cooking oil like butter, avocado, coconut or animal fat like beef tallow or lard to the inner pot and add food you want to cook like a skillet or pan. The sauté button can be used to cook ingredients like onion, garlic and meat. Most times, I start with the "Sauté" function and then use the "Manual" / "Pressure" button to pressure cook my meal.

3. **Slow Cook Button:**

    This button helps you to use Instant Pot like a slower cooker. This function allows the Instant Pot to perform the function of a slow cooker. Just add food as you normally do to a slow cooker, secure the lid and then select the "Slow Cook" button and use "+/-" buttons to adjust the cook time.

4. **Bean / Chili:**

    This button allows the Instant Pot to cook beans faster than any other cooker. This is why beans is the food I like cooking most in my Instant Pot. The "Bean / Chili" button, uses the default High Pressure for 30 minutes though it can be adjusted for "More" to High Pressure for 35 minutes or "Less" for High Pressure for 20 minutes. Black beans take about 10-15 minutes, while kidney beans take 20-25. The Instant Pot Manual has different cooking times for various beans and legumes.

5. **Meat / Stew:**

    The Instant Pot can easily make your favorite stew or meat dish. It can make it by adjusting the settings depending on the desired texture. For instance, a homemade stew with about 1-2 lb. of meat, you can set it to "Meat / Stew" button using high pressure for 35 minutes. The "More" setting is great for fall-off-the-bone cooking. It will set to a default

High Pressure for 35 minutes. The Instant Pot can be adjusted for "More" to High Pressure for 45 minutes or "Less" for High Pressure for 20 minutes.

6. **Multigrain:**

This function can be used for cooking wild rice or brown rice which usually takes longer time than cooking white rice. Cook brown rice to a 1:1.25 ratio rice to water and wild rice to a 1:3 ratio rice to water for 25-30 minutes. The default (Normal) setting is 40 minutes of cooking time but can be adjusted as required for the "Less" setting to 20 minutes of cooking time, or "More" at 45 minutes of warm water soaking and 60 minutes of cooking.

7. **Porridge:**

Rice porridge (congee) and other grains can be cooked using the porridge button.

The default cooking time on High Pressure for rice porridge is 20 minutes but can be adjusted for "More" to High Pressure for 30 minutes or "Less" for High Pressure for 15 minutes. When the cooking cycle has completed, it is not advisable to use Quick Pressure Release because it has high starch content and may splatter the porridge through the steam release vent. It's imperative to use the Natural Pressure Release to release the steam.

8. **Poultry:**

This button can be used for making chicken and other poultry recipes in the Instant Pot. The default cooking program is 15 minutes but can be adjusted for "More" to High Pressure for 30 minutes or "Less" for High Pressure for 5 minutes. I always make shredded chicken for homemade tacos and burrito bowls. Add about 1 lb. uncooked chicken, ¼ cup of homemade salsa, 1 cup of bone broth, 1 tsp. cumin, 1 clove garlic minced, ½ tsp oregano, ½ onion, and $1/8$ tsp. paprika into the bottom of your Instant Pot. Secure the lid in place and select the "Poultry" button to the default at High Pressure for 15 minutes. When the cooking cycle has finished, do a Natural Pressure Release for 10 minutes. Carefully open the lid, shred the chicken the two forks, add pepper and salt to taste.

9. **Rice:**

This button is used to cook rice in your Instant Pot using half the time a conventional rice cooker could use. It uses about 4 to 8 minutes, short grain, Jasmine, White rice, and Basmati rice can all be cooked using this function. You'll need a 1:1 ratio of rice to water (Basmati is a 1:1.5 ratio). It depends on the quantity of food you want to cook on low pressure, when you press the "Rice" button, the cooking duration automatically adjusts. It's always necessary to add further 10-12 minutes to the cooking time to allow the Instant Pot to come to pressure but cooking rice in the "Manual" mode at high pressure is my frequent selection. I usually add 1:1 ratio of rice to water into the bottom of my Instant Pot and set to 3 minutes with a 12 minutes Natural Pressure Release when the timer beeps.

10. **Soup:**

Soup, stock, and broth can be made using the "Soup" button. Water doesn't heavily boil because Instant Pot will control the pressure and temperature so that the liquid doesn't heavily boil. You can adjust the cooking time as required, usually between 20-40 minutes, and the pressure to either Low or High Pressure. Anytime you wish to make homemade bone broth faster than the conventional slow cooker, it is very simple. Click the "Soup" button, set the Low Pressure, and set the cooking time to 120 minutes. Once the timer beeps, do Natural Pressure Release to release the steam.

11. **Steam:**

This button can be used to steam vegetables, seafood or reheat food. Always use the steam rack of your Instant Pot when steaming veggies to avoid burning and sticking to the bottom of your Instant Pot. Add 1-2 cups of water to the inner liner, place the steam rack inside the inner pot and with a stainless steel steam basket on top. Add the vegetables, seafood, etc. in the basket. Select the "Steam" button and then adjust the time using the "+" or "-" key. When you are cooking foods like frozen corn on the cob or a fresh fish filet, adjust the time to 3-5 minutes and 8-10 minutes if you are cooking fresh artichokes could take 9-11 minutes.

12. **Keep Warm Button:**

This button is used to keep food hot when the Instant Pot is done with cooking or to cancel the pressure cooking mode. Immediately cooking time is finished, the Instant Pot will beep and automatically go into the "Keep Warm" function. It will display an "L" in front of a number to indicate how long it's been warm – e.g. "L0:30" for 30 minutes. This button helps to keep food warm (145 to 172°F) for up to 99 hours, 50 minutes.

13. **Cancel Button:**

If by mistake you selected wrong cooking time and you want to stop cooking or adjust pressure cooking time, you can cancel and return to standby mode by selecting the "Keep Warm" / "Cancel" button.

14. **Timer Button**

This button can be used to delay the cooking start time for the Instant Pot for both pressure cooking and slow cook options. Press the Timer button with 10 seconds of pressing Pressure / Manual button or Slow Cook button. To adjust the delayed hours, Use "+/-" buttons then wait a second and press Timer again to set delayed minutes. Press the Keep Warm / Cancel button to cancel the Timer anytime

Step-By-Step Guide to Clean Your Instant Pot

Step 1: Unplug:

Prior to start cleaning your Instant Pot, ensure that your Instant Pot is unplugged. It's advisable to unplug your Instant Pot whenever it's not in use. Always unplugged your Instant Pot whenever you want to clean it for the safety of your Instant Pot and for your safety too.

Step 2: Cleaning housing unit:

Clean outside the housing unit with a rag because it cannot be placed on dishwater. Get the rag good and damp with water and add a cleaning solution. Clean both the interior and exterior parts of the main housing unit with the rag. A sponge is recommended to have a perfect cleaning in other to remove those hard or stiff food bits and mineral deposits stuck into the housing unit.

Step 3: Wash the lid:

The lid can properly be washed with warm water. It should be washed in the sink with warm water and a little dish soap to remove all the residuals that can contaminate your food. Some people use a vinegar solution to remove the unpleasant smell from residuals.

Step 4: Check other crevices:

The Instant Pot has some parts that you might not like to clean all the time you are washing the Instant Pot. Get all those crevices and small parts where food residue may stuck to the parts for some period of time. Remove the Quick Pressure Release handle, and wash it with warm-soapy water. The steam valve can be blocked if too much deposit are stuck there. Remove the shield, located inside the lid which blocks the valve and wash them in the sink.

Step 5: Clean sealing ring:

The silicone ring found on the underside of the lid requires to be thoroughly cleaned to avoid changing the taste of your food. This implies that the Instant Pot has a tight seal, and it's an easy spot for food particles or residual smells to lurk. Check the silicone seal for any signs of damage, because silicone has the tendency to begin cracking over time. If you notice any crack in the silicone ring, it has been damaged and needs a replacement immediately. The silicone ring can be washed in dish water because it is dishwasher-safe. Place the silicone ring into your Instant Pot after washing.

Step 6: Wash the inner pot:

The inner pot is dishwasher-safe. The inner pot should be washed in dish water regularly. Place the inner pot into the dishwasher together with any of the other dishwasher-safe parts you use with your Instant Pot, such as silicone molds and wire racks. After washing the inner pot, pat it dry with a clean paper towel or some household vinegar dry it off. The reason for drying it is to get rid of any accumulated residue from things like minerals in your water, or dish detergent.

Step 7: Steam clean and pat dry:

This is the final stage of cleaning your Instant Pot. At this stage, you must have done a thorough cleaning, all you need to do is to reassemble all the parts of your Instant Pot. Don't forget about those small parts like the sealing ring and shield because they can be missed easily. The aim of washing and cleaning is to ensure your Instant Pot is safe it can last for a long period of time. However, after doing all the washing and cleaning but you realized the sealing ring still has a strange food smell, you just need to deodorize the sealing ring with a vinegar steam clean to remove the strange smell. The process is simple and can be done directly in the Instant Pot by adding a cup of water, a cup of vinegar, and some lemon peels (to add extra freshness!) to the inner pot, press "Steam" function and set for a couple of minutes. When the timer beeps, do a natural pressure release. Carefully remove the lid, remove the sealing ring and dry it off.

INSTANT POT BREAKFAST RECIPES

Breakfast Cobbler

Preparation time: 10 minutes

Cook time: 15 minutes

Total time: 25 minutes

Serves: 2

Ingredients:

- 1 pear, diced
- 1 apple, diced
- 1 plum, diced
- 2 tablespoons (30 ml) local honey
- 3 tablespoons (45 ml) coconut oil
- ½ teaspoon of ground cinnamon
- ¼ cup (19 g) of unsweetened shredded coconut
- ¼ cup (30 g) of pecan pieces
- 2 tablespoons (20 g) of sunflower seeds (salted and roasted will be great too)
- Optional garnish: Coconut whipped cream

Cooking Instructions:

1. Add the cut fruit into the stainless steel bowl of your Instant Pot.
2. Spoon in the honey and coconut oil, sprinkle the cinnamon. Close and lock the lid in place and ensure that the valve is in sealing position.
3. Select the Steam function; the display will read 10 minutes. Allow the fruit to cook. When the timer beeps, do a quick pressure release.
4. Carefully open the lid and transfer the cooked fruit with a slotted spoon into a serving plate.
5. Add the coconut, pecans, and sunflower seeds into the residual liquid and select the Sauté function. Allow the contents to cook, turning them regularly to avoid burning.
6. When they are nicely browned and toasted for about 5 minutes, remove them and top your cooked fruit.
7. Serve hot and topped with coconut whipped cream if desired.

Pumpkin Spice Latte Oats

Preparation time: 10 minutes

Cook time: 20 minutes

Total time: 30 minutes

Servings: 2-4

Ingredients:

- 1 cup of steel cut oats
- 2 cups of water
- 1 cup of milk
- ½ cup of pumpkin puree
- 1 tsp. of pumpkin pie spice
- A dash of salt
- A dash of black pepper
- ¼ cup of brown sugar
- 2 tbsp. of vanilla
- ½ cup of strong coffee
- ¼ cup of half and half or heavy cream

Cooking Instructions:

1. In a medium bowl, combine together the oats, water, and milk.
2. Pour the mixture into the bottom of your Instant Pot. Close and lock the lid in place. Select Manual, High Pressure for 12 minutes.
3. Select Multigrain Less, if using an Instant Pot. When the cooking cycle has completed, do a natural pressure release for about 5 minutes, then release any remaining pressure.
4. Carefully open the lid and stir in pumpkin, pumpkin pie spice, salt, pepper, brown sugar, vanilla, and coffee.
5. Ladle into a bowl, top with some extra brown sugar and a drizzle of heavy cream if desired.
6. Serve and enjoy!

Crustless Tomato Spinach Quiche

Preparation time: 10 minutes

Cook time: 20 minutes

Total time: 30 minutes

Servings: 6

Ingredients:

- 12 large eggs
- ½ cup of milk
- ½ tsp. of salt
- ¼ tsp. of fresh ground black pepper
- 3 cups of fresh baby spinach, chopped
- 1 cup of diced seeded tomato
- 3 large green onions, sliced
- 4 tomato slices, for topping
- ¼ cup of shredded Parmesan cheese

Cooking Instructions:

1. Place the trivet into the bottom of your Instant Pot and pour 1 ½ cups of water.
2. In a medium bowl, whisk together the eggs, milk, salt and pepper. Add the spinach, tomato, and green onions to a 1 ½ quart baking dish and give everything a good mix.
3. Add your egg mixture over the veggies and give everything a good stir to combine. Gently add the sliced tomatoes on top and sprinkle with Parmesan cheese.
4. Place the dish on the trivet with a sling. Close and lock the lid in place. Select Manual, High Pressure for 20 minutes.
5. When the time is up, do a natural pressure release for 10 minutes, then quick release any remaining pressure.
6. Carefully remove the lid, take out the dish and broil for a couple of minutes until lightly browned if desired.
7. Serve and enjoy!

Berries and Cream Breakfast Cake

Servings: 6

Ingredients:

Breakfast Cake:

- 5 eggs
- ¼ cup of sugar
- 2 tbsp. butter, melted
- ¾ cup of ricotta cheese
- ¾ cup of plain or vanilla yogurt
- 2 tsp. of vanilla extract
- 1 cup of whole wheat pastry flour or white whole wheat flour
- ½ tsp. of salt
- 2 tsp. of baking powder
- ½ cup of Berry Compote
- Sweet Yogurt Glaze
- Berry Compote (prepare and chill beforehand)

Sweet Yogurt Glaze:

- ¼ cup of yogurt
- ½ tsp. of vanilla extract
- 1 tsp. of milk
- 1-2 tsp. of powdered sugar

Cooking Instructions:

1. Make the Berry Compote beforehand to be cold and thick. It has a tendency to sink to the pan if used war.
2. For the Breakfast Cake, use a nonstick cooking spray to grease a 6 cup Bundt pan. Beat together the eggs and sugar until smooth.
3. Add together the butter, ricotta cheese, yogurt, and vanilla and give everything a good mix until smooth. In a medium bowl, whisk together the flour, salt, and baking powder.
4. Add the mixture to combine with the egg mixture. Pour into the prepared Bundt pan. Using ½ cup of Berry Compote, drop by tablespoons on top of the batter and swirl in with a knife.
5. Pour 1 cup of water into the bottom of your Instant Pot and add the trivet. Carefully place the Bundt pan on the trivet.
6. Close and lock the lid in place and ensure that the valve is in sealing position. Select Manual, High Pressure for 25 minutes.

7. While the cake is cooking, prepare the Sweet Yogurt Glaze by whisking together the yogurt, vanilla, milk, and powdered sugar and keep aside.
8. When the timer beeps, do a natural pressure release for about 10 minutes, then quick release any remaining pressure.
9. Carefully open the lid and remove the Bundt pan from your Instant Pot. Allow to cool and loosen the edges of the cake from the pan.
10. Flip over onto a plate and drizzle with Sweet Yogurt Glaze.
11. Serve warm and enjoy!

Mushroom Risotto

Servings: 5 ½ cups

Preparation time: 10 minutes

Cook time: 5 minutes

Total time: 15 minutes

Ingredients:

- 2 tablespoons of extra-virgin olive oil
- 1 pound of wild mushrooms, trimmed, sliced
- Pinch of kosher salt
- Freshly ground pepper
- 1 medium onion, chopped
- 2 cups of carnaroli or arborio rice
- ½ cup of white wine
- 4 ½ cups of vegetable or chicken stock
- Chopped parsley, for serving
- Finely grated Parmesan (for serving)

Cooking Instructions:

1. Press the "Sauté" button on your Instant Pot and add the oil.
2. Add the mushrooms and sauté until the moisture is evaporated and they begin to brown, for about 10 minutes. Generously season with salt and pepper.
3. Add onion and give everything a good stir to combine. Cook the contents until translucent for about 8 minutes. Add the rice and stir until chalky white for about 3 minutes.
4. Add the wine and cook for about 3 minutes until almost evaporated. Close and lock the lid in place and ensure that the valve is in sealing position.
5. Select Manual, High Pressure for 5 minutes. When the timer beeps, do a quick pressure release. Carefully remove the lid and stir with a wooden spoon.
6. Season with salt and pepper to taste. Divide risotto among serving plates. Top with parsley and Parmesan if desired and serve immediately.

Hidden Cauliflower Mac 'n' Cheese

Serves: 8

Preparation time: 10 minutes

Cook time: 3 minutes

Total time: 13 minutes

Ingredients:

- 1 lb. of whole-wheat macaroni
- 4 cups of water
- 2 tbsp. of soy sauce or tamari
- 1 tbsp. of spicy brown mustard
- 1 ½ tsp. of fine sea salt
- 1 lb. of fresh or frozen cauliflower florets
- 4 oz. extra-sharp Cheddar
- ¼ cup of grated Parmesan cheese, or your desired cheese, like gruyere

Cooking Instructions:

1. Add the pasta into the bottom of your Instant Pot and pour the water, soy sauce, mustard, and salt.
2. Give everything a good stir to combine. Add the cauliflower on top without stirring, and ensure that the cauliflower layer is completely submerged the pasta.
3. Close and lock the lid in place. Select Manual, High Pressure for 3 minutes. Shred the Cheddar while the pot is cooking.
4. When the timer beeps, do a natural pressure release fir about 10 minutes, then quick release any remaining pressure.
5. Carefully open the lid and give the pasta a good stir with a spatula to break up any pasta that has stuck together.
6. Mash the cauliflower florets against the side of the pot to help them dissolve into the pasta sauce. Add the Cheddar and parmesan and give everything a good stir.
7. Adjust the seasonings to suit your desired taste. Serve warm and enjoy!

Breakfast Burritos

Preparation time: 10 minutes

Cook time: 25 minutes

Total time: 35 minutes

Ingredients:

- 2 ½ cups of O'Brien hash browns
- 1 cup of diced ham (or your desired protein)
- 6 eggs
- ¼ cup of milk
- ¼ cup of sour cream
- ½ cup of shredded cheese
- ¼ teaspoon of salt
- 1/8 teaspoon of pepper

Cooking Instructions:

1. Use a non-stick cooking spray to spray the inner liner of your Instant Pot. Measure out and add the hash browns into the bottom of the Instant Pot liner.
2. Pour the ham (or your desired protein) on top of the frozen hash browns. In a small bowl, whisk together the eggs, milk, sour cream shredded cheese, salt and pepper.
3. Pour the eggs into the small liner on top of the hash browns and protein. Tightly cover the liner with a piece of foil.
4. In the large liner, add 1 cup of water into the bottom and then place the trivet inside of the liner. Add the small 'inner pot' inside of the large pot, onto the trivet.
5. Close and lock the lid in place and ensure that the valve is in sealing position. Select Manual, High Pressure for 25 minutes.
6. When the timer beeps, do a quick pressure release. Carefully remove the lid and remove the foil, stir and then replace the foil.
7. Close and lock the lid in place. Cook again on Manual, High Pressure for 10 minutes. When the timer beeps, do a quick pressure release.
8. It is now ready to be stuffed into tortillas to make delicious breakfast burritos! Serve and enjoy.

Vanilla Latte Steel Cut Oats

Servings: 4

Preparation time: 10 minutes

Cook time: 10 minutes

Total time: 20 minutes

Ingredients:

- 2 ½ cups of water
- 1 cup of milk
- 1 cup of steel cut oats
- 2 tbsp. of sugar
- 1 tsp. of espresso powder
- ¼ tsp. of salt
- 2 tsp. of vanilla extract
- Freshly whipped cream
- Finely grated chocolate

Cooking Instructions:

1. Pour the water, milk, oats, sugar, espresso powder, and salt into the bottom of your Instant Pot.
2. Give everything a good stir to dissolve espresso powder. Close and lock the lid in place and ensure that the valve is in sealing position.
3. Select Manual, High Pressure for 10 minutes. When the timer beeps, do a natural pressure release for about 10 minutes, then quick release any remaining pressure.
4. Carefully open the lid and stir in vanilla extract and additional sugar to taste. Cover and allow to sit for about 5 minutes until your desired thickness of the oats is achieved.
5. Serve topped with whipped cream and grated chocolate.

Macaroni and Cheese

Servings: 6

Preparation time: 10 minutes

Cook time: 6 minutes

Total time: 16 minutes

Ingredients:

- 1 lb. of elbow macaroni
- 4 cups of low-sodium chicken broth or vegetable broth
- 3 tbsp. of unsalted butter
- 12 oz. of shredded sharp Cheddar cheese (3 cups tightly packed)
- ½ cup of shredded Parmesan cheese (about 2 oz.)
- ½ cup of sour cream
- 1 ½ tsp. of prepared yellow mustard
- 1/8 tsp. of cayenne pepper

Cooking Instructions:

1. In a medium bowl, combine together the macaroni, broth, and butter.
2. Pour the mixture into the bottom of your Instant Pot.
3. Close and lock the lid in place and ensure that the valve is in sealing position.
4. Select the Manual, High Pressure for 6 minutes. When the timer beeps, do a quick pressure release.
5. Carefully remove the lid and stir in the cheeses, sour cream, mustard, and cayenne pepper.
6. Allow it to sit for about 5 minutes to thicken, then stir again.
7. Serve and enjoy!

Buckwheat Porridge

Preparation time: 5 minutes

Cook time: 25 minutes

Total time: 30 minutes

Servings: 4

Ingredients:

- 1 cup of raw buckwheat groats
- 3 cups of rice milk
- 1 banana, sliced
- ¼ cup of raisins
- 1 teaspoon of ground cinnamon
- ½ teaspoon of vanilla
- Chopped nuts, optional

Cooking Instructions:

1. Rinse the buckwheat and add into the bottom of your Instant Pot.
2. Add the rice milk, banana, raisins, cinnamon and vanilla. Close and lock the lid in place and ensure that the valve is in sealing position.
3. Select Manual, High Pressure for 6 minutes. When the timer beeps, do a natural pressure release for about 20 minutes.
4. Carefully remove the lid and stir the porridge. Add more rice milk to individual servings to achieve preferred consistency.
5. Sprinkle with chopped nuts if desired and serve immediately.

Caldo Verde

Servings: 6

Preparation time: 10 minutes

Cook time: 6 minutes

Total time: 16 minutes

Ingredients:

- ¼ cup of extra-virgin olive oil
- 12 ounces of dry-cured Spanish chorizo or linguiça, casing removed, sliced into 1/4-inch rounds
- 1 bunch curly kale, stems removed and thinly sliced, leaves torn into bite-size pieces
- 2 pounds of Yukon Gold potatoes, cut into 1" pieces
- 1 onion, chopped
- 2 garlic cloves, chopped
- 1 teaspoon of kosher salt
- ¼ teaspoon of freshly ground black pepper
- 2 bay leaves

Cooking Instructions:

1. Add the oil into bottom of your Instant Pot and press the "Sauté" button.
2. Once it's hot, add the sausage and sauté, stirring frequently, until browned for about 5 minutes.
3. Drain the excess fat, add the kale, potatoes, onion, and garlic, and give everything a good stir to coat. Generously season with salt and pepper to taste.
4. Add the bay leaves and pour 6 cups water. Give everything a good stir to combine. Press the Cancel button.
5. Close and lick the lid in place and ensure that the valve is in sealing position. Select Manual, High Pressure for 6 minutes.
6. When the timer beeps, do a quick pressure release. Carefully remove the lid and add more salt to taste.
7. Serve and enjoy!

Brown Butter Steel-Cut Oatmeal

Serves: 4

Preparation time: 10 minutes

Cook time: 12 minutes

Total time: 22 minutes

Ingredients:

- 2 tbsp. of unsalted butter
- 1 ½ cups of steel-cut oats
- 4 ½ cups of water
- ½ tsp. of kosher salt
- Brown sugar, for serving
- Heavy cream, for serving

Cooking Instructions:

1. Press the Sauté function on the Instant Pot and add the butter.
2. Add the oats and cook, stirring often, for about 5 minutes, until lightly toasted. Pour the water and salt.
3. Give everything a good stir to combine and ensure that the oats are completely submerged in the liquid.
4. Close and lock the lid in place and ensure that the valve is in sealing position. Press the Porridge button and set the cooking time for 12 minutes at high pressure.
5. When the timer beeps, do a natural pressure release for 10 minutes, then quick release any remaining pressure.
6. Carefully open the lid and stir the oatmeal to incorporate any extra liquid. Ladle the oatmeal into plates.
7. Serve with brown sugar and cream if desired and enjoy.

INSTANT POT SOUP & STEW RECIPES

Vietnamese Chicken Noodle Soup

Servings: 4

Preparation time: 10 minutes

Cook time: 15 minutes

Total time: 25 minutes

Ingredients:

- 2 tbsp. of canola oil
- 2 medium yellow onions, halved
- 1 (2-inch) piece ginger, cut into 1/4-inch slices
- 1 tbsp. of coriander seeds
- 3 star anise pods
- 5 cloves
- 1 cinnamon stick
- 3 cardamom pods, lightly smashed
- 6 bone-in, skin-on chicken thighs
- 3 tbsp. of fish sauce
- 1 tbsp. of sugar
- 8 cups water
- Pinch of kosher salt
- Freshly ground black pepper
- 4 servings rice noodles, prepared according to package directions

Toppings:

- 3 scallions, sliced
- 1 small handful fresh herbs, such as mint, cilantro, and Thai basil, chopped
- 1 lime, cut into wedges
- Handful of bean sprouts, optional
- 1 jalapeño, thinly sliced, optional

Cooking Instructions:

1. Press the Sauté button on your Instant Pot. When hot, add the canola oil.
2. Add the onions, cut side down, and the ginger. Sauté for about 4 minutes until charred. Add the coriander, star anise, cloves, cinnamon stick, and cardamom.

3. Give everything a good stir and cook for additional 1 minute. Add the chicken, fish sauce, and sugar and pour over the water.
4. Close and lock the lid in place and ensure that the valve is in sealing position. Select Manual, High Pressure for 15 minutes.
5. When the timer beeps, do a natural pressure release for about 10 minutes, then quick release any remaining pressure.
6. Carefully open the lid and remove the chicken from the Instant Pot. Carefully strain the broth and season with salt and pepper to taste.
7. Add the cooked noodles in 4 bowls. When the chicken has cooled, shred the chicken with two forks and remove the bones.
8. Add the shredded chicken to the bowls. Pour over the broth and top with scallions, herbs, lime, and bean sprouts and jalapeño (if desired).
9. Serve and enjoy!

Italian Beef Stew

Preparation time: 10 minutes

Cook time: 35 minutes

Total time: 45 minutes

Servings: 6-8

Ingredients:

- 3 pounds of beef stew meat OR 2 pounds of ground beef, browned.
- 1 onion, diced
- 4 carrots, sliced
- 8 ounces fresh baby portabella mushrooms (optional)
- 24 ounces beef broth
- 15 ounces can diced tomatoes
- 3 tablespoons of flour
- 1 teaspoon of dried basil leaves
- 1 teaspoon of dried thyme leaves
- 1 teaspoon of salt
- 1 teaspoon of pepper dried parsley

Cooking Instructions:

1. Add the meat into the bottom of your Instant Pot. If using ground beef, sauté then drain grease.
2. Add the carrots, broth, flour, basil, thyme, salt, pepper and diced tomatoes to Instant Pot and give everything a good stir.
3. Close and lock the lid in place. Select Manual, High Pressure for 35 minutes. When the timer beeps, do a quick pressure release.
4. Carefully remove the lid and stir in mushrooms. Give everything a good stir
5. Serve and enjoy!

Vegetable Soup

Servings: 6 – 8

Preparation time: 10 minutes

Cook time: 30 minutes

Total time: 40 minutes

Ingredients:

- 2 stalks celery, chopped
- 6 carrots, chopped
- ½ medium onion, chopped
- 12 ounces frozen okra
- 12 ounces frozen green beans
- 12 ounces frozen corn
- 12 ounces frozen peas
- 4 cups beef broth

Cooking Instructions:

1. Add all the chopped and frozen veggies into the bottom of your Instant Pot.
2. Pour the beef broth into your Instant Pot. Use either broth you've saved from a roast, or a beef base or bullion to make a broth.
3. Substitute the beef broth with a vegetable broth if you are a vegetarian. Close and lock the lid in place.
4. Select "Soup" button to cook for 30 minutes. When the timer beeps, do a natural pressure release. Carefully open the lid and stir.
5. Serve warm and enjoy!

Italian Sausage Stew

Preparation time: 10 minutes

Cook time: 3 minutes

Total time: 13 minutes

Ingredients:

- 2 tablespoons of butter
- ½ pound of pastured ground pork (grass fed ground beef would be great too)
- ½ teaspoon of onion powder
- ½ teaspoon of garlic powder
- 1½ teaspoon of basil
- ½ teaspoon of thyme
- ¼ teaspoon of cumin
- ½ teaspoon of marjoram
- ¼ teaspoon of cayenne
- 1 teaspoon of sea salt
- ¼ teaspoon of black pepper
- 1 medium onion, diced
- 2 carrots, diced
- 2 stalks of celery, diced
- 4 cloves of garlic, minced
- ½ cup white wine
- 1 – 15 ounces can organic diced tomatoes
- 2 quarts bone broth
- 2-3 large handfuls kale, chopped
- 8 ounces gluten free noodles
- Sea salt/pepper to taste
- Freshly grated parm or other raw cheese to garnish

Cooking Instructions:

1. Press the "Sauté" function on your Instant Pot and add the butter to melt.
2. Add the pork and all of the seasonings.
3. Give everything a good stir to combine and brown the meat.
4. Add the onion, carrot, celery, and garlic, and stir to combine.
5. Cook the veggies for about 5 to 7 minutes or until they have softened.
6. Deglaze the pan with white wine scraping up any bits at the bottom.
7. Add the diced tomatoes, broth, kale and noodles and give everything a good stir to combine.
8. Close and lock the lid in place.

9. Select Manual, High Pressure for 3 minutes. When the timer beeps, do a quick pressure release.
10. Carefully open the lid and season with salt and pepper to taste.
11. Serve with freshly grated parmesan and enjoy!

Cheddar Broccoli & Potato Soup

Servings: 4- 6

Preparation time: 10 minutes

Cook time: 15 minutes

Total time: 25 minutes

Ingredients:

- 2 tablespoons of butter
- 2 cloves garlic, crushed
- 1 medium sized broccoli head, broken into large florets
- 2 pounds Yukon Gold Potatoes, peeled and cut into small chunks
- 4 cups of vegetable or chicken broth, plus more if required
- Salt to taste
- Pepper to taste
- 1 cup of half and half
- 1 cup of shredded cheddar cheese
- 6 slices of bacon (optional)
- Chopped green onion or chives for garnish

Cooking Instructions:

1. Press the Sauté button on your Instant Pot and add the butter to melt.
2. Add the add butter and crushed garlic. Cook for about 2 minutes, or until garlic starts to brown. Add the broccoli, potatoes, and broth.
3. Generously season with extra salt and pepper. Close and lock the lid in place and ensure that the valve is in sealing position.
4. Select Manual, High Pressure for 5 minutes. When the timer beeps, do a natural pressure release for about 10 minutes, then quick release any remaining pressure.
5. If using bacon, microwave or cook the bacon until your desired crispiness is achieved and set aside to cool. Add the half and half and ½ cup of cheddar cheese.
6. Use an immersion blender to blend until smooth. Add more broth if you desire a thinner soup. Add salt and pepper to taste.
7. Serve warm with remaining cheddar and bacon (if desired) and enjoy.

Ham Gnocchi Soup

Preparation time: 10 minutes

Cook time: 4 minutes

Total time: 14 minutes

Ingredients:

- ½ stick of butter
- 1 tbsp. of oil
- 1 cup of onion
- 2 tbsp. of garlic
- ½ cup of celery
- ¾ of shredded carrots
- 1 cup of coarsely chopped fresh spinach leaves
- 1 quart of half and half
- Package of gnocchi
- 2 cups of ham or chicken
- ½ cup of flour
- 28 ounces of chicken broth

Spices:

- ¼ tsp. of parsley flakes
- ½ tsp. of thyme
- Salt and pepper

Cooking Instructions:

1. Press the Sauté button on your Instant Pot and add the oil and butter. Add the onion and sauté until the onions are translucent.
2. Add the flour and cook for additional 1 minute. Add in your half and half and give everything a good stir to get thicker.
3. Add the broth, salt, pepper, the thyme, parsley, carrots, spinach, chicken, and gnocchi into the pot. Close and lock the lid in place.
4. Select Manual, High Pressure for 4 minutes. When the timer beeps, do a quick pressure release. Carefully open the lid and stir.
5. Serve and enjoy!

Spanish Infused Chicken Stew

Preparation time: 10 minutes

Cook time: 3 hours

Total time: 3 hours 10 minutes

Ingredients:

- 4 large chicken breasts, cut into chunks
- 4 cloves of garlic, minced
- ½ cooking chorizo, roughly chopped
- 2 carrots, chopped roughly
- 2 courgettes, roughly chopped
- 2 leeks, roughly chopped
- 3 red skinned potatoes, scrubbed and chopped in half
- 1 can of cannellini beans
- 1 handful of parsley, roughly chopped
- Handful of oregano, finely chopped
- A glass of fino sherry or dry white wine, and one for yourself
- Pinch of smoked paprika
- A couple of strands of saffron
- Salt and pepper to taste
- Chicken stock, enough to cover the chicken and vegetables

Cooking Instructions:

1. Prepare the vegetables and add them into the bottom of your Instant Pot.
2. Heat a few tablespoons of oil in a sauté pan and sauté the garlic, chicken and chorizo until the chicken is browned.
3. Add the chicken, chorizo and garlic mixture into the bottom of your Instant Pot and give everything a good stir.
4. Lightly heat the stock and add the herbs, spices and seasonings. Pour the contents over the chicken and ensure that the chicken is covered with the broth.
5. Close and lock the lid in place and ensure that the valve is in sealing position. Select Slow Cook for 3 hours.
6. When the timer beeps, do a quick pressure release. Carefully open the lid and adjust the seasoning to taste. Ladle from the pot into serving plates.
7. Serve with crusty bread or rice and enjoy!

Chicken Noodle Soup

Servings: 4 - 6

Ingredients:

- 3 tbsp. of salted butter
- 1 ¼ cups of onion, chopped
- 4 cloves garlic, chopped
- 1 ¼ cups of carrots, chopped
- 1 ¼ cups celery, chopped
- 1 lb. of chicken, cooked and chopped
- 4 cups of chicken broth
- 1 package home-style noodles
- Pinch of celery salt, optional

Cooking Instructions:

1. Add the chicken in your Instant Pot and cook beforehand. Remove the chicken and set aside.
2. Press the Sauté button and add the butter to melt. Cook all the vegetables for about 2-3 minutes, or until soft.
3. Add in chopped chicken and broth, and give everything a good stir. Add the noodles.
4. Close and lock the lid in place. Cook the noodles until your desired doneness is achieved.
5. Carefully open the lid and add a pinch of celery salt, if desired.
6. Serve and enjoy!

Tomato Chick Pea Soup

Preparation time: 10 minutes

Cook time: 3 minutes

Total time: 13 minutes

Ingredients:

- 3 tbsp. of olive oil
- 2 onions, diced
- 3 celery stalks, diced
- 3 carrots, diced
- 1 red bell pepper, diced
- 1 tbsp. of turmeric
- 1 tbsp. of ground coriander
- 1 tsp. of ground cinnamon
- 1 garlic clove, minced
- 28-30 oz. of canned or fresh tomatoes
- 1 zucchini
- 2-3 cups of broth (vegetable or bone)
- 2 cans chickpeas (garbanzo beans)
- A pinch of salt
- Freshly grounded pepper
- Garnish with Lime wedges, green onions or cilantro (optional)

Cooking Instructions:

1. Select the Sauté function on your Instant Pot and add the butter and oil.
2. Add the onions and carrots and cook for about 4 to 6 minutes or until the onions become translucent. Add the celery and red bell pepper, along with the dry spices.
3. Stir in the garlic, tomatoes, and zucchini. Rinse the chickpeas and add to mixture. Add enough broth to cover vegetables and reserve some broth.
4. Season with Salt and Pepper to taste. Press Cancel function. Close and lock the lid in place and ensure that the valve is in sealing position.
5. Select Manual, High Pressure for 3 minutes. When the timer beeps, do a quick pressure release. Carefully open the lid and give everything a good stir.
6. Add more broth if desired. Squeeze the lime over the top or offer lime wedges with soup plates just before serving. Serve and enjoy!

Creamy Thai Coconut Chicken Soup

Serves: 4

Preparation time: 5 minutes

Cook time: 6 minutes

Total time: 11 minutes

Ingredients:

- 2 tbsp. of oil
- 1 medium onion, quartered
- 2 pound of skinless and boneless chicken breast or chicken thighs, cut into cubes
- 2 tbsp. of Thai red curry paste (Mae Ploy brand)
- 1 red bell pepper, cut into thick strips
- 6 slices galangal, optional
- 6 kaffir lime leaves, torn and bruised, optional
- 3 cups of chicken broth
- 2 tbsp. of fish sauce or salt to taste
- 1 tbsp. of sugar
- ¾ cup of coconut milk
- 2 ½ tbsp. of lime juice
- Cilantro leaves

Cooking Instructions:

1. Select the Sauté button on your Instant Pot and add the oil. Add the onion and cook for about 10 seconds until browned.
2. Add the chicken and sauté until the surface turns white. Add the Thai curry paste, bell peppers, galangal and kaffir lime leaves (if desired), and give everything a good stir to mix.
3. Add the chicken broth, fish sauce and sugar. Close and lock the lid in place and ensure that the valve is in sealing position.
4. Select Manual, High Pressure for 6 minutes. When the timer beeps, do a quick pressure release. Carefully open the lid and add the coconut milk.
5. Add the lime juice to the soup, and give everything a good stir to combine. Top with cilantro and serve immediately.

Smoky Lentil and Potato Soup

Preparation time: 15 minutes

Cook time: 3 minutes

Total time: 18 minutes

Ingredients:

- 1 tbsp. of olive oil
- ½ cup of chopped yellow or white onion
- 3 cloves garlic, finely minced
- ½ cup of diced carrots (about 2 medium carrots)
- ½ cup of diced celery (about 2 stalks)
- 2 tsp. of ground cumin
- 1 ½ tsp. of smoked paprika
- 1 tsp. of salt
- 1 lb. of Yukon Gold or red potatoes, cut into 1-inch pieces
- 1 cup of red lentils, sorted and rinsed
- 1 cup of brown lentils, sorted and rinsed
- 8 cups of chicken or vegetable stock or broth
- 8 - 10 oz. of kale or spinach, chopped (optional)

Cooking Instructions:

1. Press the Sauté button on your Instant Pot and add the oil.
2. When hot, add the onion, garlic, carrots, and celery, and sauté for a couple of minutes, stirring constantly to avoid burning the garlic.
3. Add the cumin, paprika and salt and give everything a good stir to combine. Add the potatoes, lentils and stock or broth.
4. Close and lock the lid in place and ensure that the valve is in sealing position. Select Manual, High Pressure for 3 minutes.
5. When the timer beeps, do a quick pressure release. Carefully open the lid and stir in the kale or spinach, if desired.
6. Generously season with salt and pepper to taste. Allow the soup to cool before serving.
7. Serve and enjoy!

INSTANT POT FISH & SEAFOOD RECIPES

Shrimp Scampi

Servings: 4

Preparation time: 10 minutes

Cook time: 1 minute

Total time: 11 minutes

Ingredients:

- 1 ½ pound of jumbo shrimp, peeled, deveined
- ¼ cup of dry white wine
- 4 garlic cloves, finely chopped
- 2 teaspoons of kosher salt
- ¼ teaspoon of freshly ground black pepper
- 6 tablespoons of unsalted butter
- ¼ cup of finely chopped parsley
- 2 teaspoons of fresh lemon juice

Cooking Instructions:

1. Add the shrimp, wine, and garlic into the bottom of your Instant Pot.
2. Season with salt and pepper. Close and lock the lid in place and ensure that the valve is in sealing position.
3. Select Manual, High Pressure for 1 minute. When the timer beeps, do a quick pressure release.
4. Carefully open the lid and transfer the shrimp to a small bowl with a slotted spoon, leaving juices behind.
5. Press the "Sauté" button to simmer liquid until reduced by half for about 6 minutes.
6. Add butter and give everything a good stir until melted and incorporated and sauce is thick. Add the shrimp back to the pot, add the parsley and lemon juice.
7. Give everything a good stir to combine. Serve and enjoy!

Steamed Alaskan Crab Legs

Ingredients:

- 2-3 lbs. frozen crab legs

- 1 cup of water

- ½ tablespoon salt

- Butter, melted for serving

Cooking Instructions:

1. Place the Instant Pot insert and place steamer basket into the bottom of your Instant Pot.
2. Pour 1 cup of water and ½ tbsp. of salt. Add half of the Alaskan King Crab Legs with 1 tbsp. of salt. Close and lock the lid in place.
3. Select Manual, High Pressure for 4 minutes. When the timer beeps, do a quick pressure release.
4. Carefully open the lid and remove the crab legs. Repeat the process with remaining half of crab legs.
5. Serve with melted butter and enjoy!

10-Minute Instant Pot Salmon

Yield: 4

Preparation time: 10 minutes

Cook time: 5 minutes

Total time: 15 minutes

Ingredients:

- 3 medium lemon
- ¾ cup of water
- 4 fillet salmon
- 1 bunch dill weed, fresh
- 1 tbsp. of butter, unsalted
- ¼ tsp. of salt
- ¼ tsp. of black pepper, ground
- 1 cup of brown rice, raw
- 4 cups of green beans

Cooking Instructions:

1. Add the ¼ cup of fresh lemon juice and pour the ¾ cup of water in the bottom of your Instant Pot. Place the steamer insert.
2. Add the (Sockeye) salmon fillets, frozen, on top of the steamer insert. Sprinkle with fresh dill on top of the salmon.
3. Add 1 slice of fresh lemon on top of each one. Close and lock the lid in place. Select Manual, High Pressure for 5 minutes.
4. When the cooking cycle has completed, do a quick pressure release. Carefully open the lid and stir.
5. Serve with butter, extra dill and lemon, and salt and pepper.

Shrimp Paella

Preparation time: 10 minutes

Cook time: 5 minutes

Total time: 15 minutes

Yield: 4

Ingredients:

- 1 pound of jumbo shrimp, shell and tail on frozen
- 1 cup of Jasmine rice
- 4 tablespoons of butter
- 1 onion, chopped
- 4 cloves garlic, chopped
- 1 red pepper, chopped
- 1 cup of chicken broth
- ½ cup of white wine
- 1 teaspoon of paprika
- 1 teaspoon of turmeric
- ½ teaspoon of salt
- ¼ teaspoon of black pepper
- 1 pinch saffron threads
- ¼ teaspoon of red pepper flakes
- ¼ cup of cilantro, optional

Cooking Instructions:

1. Press the Sauté button on your Instant Pot and add the butter to melt.
2. Add the onions and sauté until softened for a couple of minutes. Add the garlic and sauté for additional 1 minute.
3. Add the paprika, turmeric, salt, black pepper, red pepper flakes, and saffron threads. Give everything a good stir and cook for additional 1 minute.
4. Add the red peppers. Add rice and stir again. Cook for about 1 minute. Add the chicken broth and white wine and ensure that the rice is covered with the broth.
5. Add shrimp on top. Press the Cancel button. Close and lock the lid in place and ensure that the valve is in sealing position. Select Manual, High Pressure for 5 minutes.
6. When the timer beeps, do a quick pressure release. Carefully open the lid and transfer the shrimp to a bowl. Peel the shrimp if desired.
7. Serve with cilantro.

Coconut Fish Curry

Preparation time: 5 minutes

Cook time: 15 minutes

Total time: 20 minutes

Ingredients:

- 1-1.5 pound (500-750g) Fish steaks or fillets, rinsed and cut into bite-size pieces (fresh or frozen and thawed)
- 1 tomato, chopped
- 2 green chilies, sliced
- 2 medium onions, sliced
- 2 Garlic cloves, squeezed
- 1 tablespoon of freshly grated ginger, (or ⅛ tsp. of ginger powder)
- 6 curry leaves, or bay laurel leaves, or kaffir lime leaves, or basil
- 1 tablespoon of ground coriander
- 2 teaspoons of ground cumin
- ½ teaspoon of ground turmeric
- 1 teaspoon of chili powder, or 1 teaspoon of Hot Pepper Flakes
- ½ teaspoon of ground Fenugreek (Methi)

OR

- 3 tablespoons of curry powder mix. (instead of the 5 spices above)
- 2 cups or (500ml) unsweetened Coconut Milk
- 2 teaspoons of salt
- Juice from ½ lemon

Cooking Instructions:

1. Press the Sauté button on your Instant Pot and add a swirl of oil.
2. Add the curry leaves and lightly fry them for about 1 minute or until golden around the edges.
3. Add the onion, garlic, and ginger and cook until the onion is soft. Add all of the ground spices: coriander, cumin, turmeric, chili powder and Fenugreek.
4. Cook the ingredients together for about 2 minutes or until they have released their aroma.
5. Deglaze the pot with coconut milk to remove any browned bits stuck to the bottom of the pot and incorporate it into the sauce.
6. Add the green chilies, tomatoes and fish pieces. Give everything a good stir to coat the fish with the mixture. Close and lock the lid in place.

7. Cook on Low Pressure for 5 minutes. When the timer beeps, do a natural pressure release for about 10 minutes.
8. Carefully open the lid and season with salt to taste. Spritz with lemon juice just before serving.
9. Serve alone, or with steamed rice if desired and enjoy.

Chipotle Shrimp Soup

Preparation time: 5 minutes

Cook time: 25 minutes

Total time: 30 minutes

Servings: 5

Ingredients:

- 3 slices bacon, chopped
- 1 cup of onion, diced
- ¾ cup of celery, chopped
- 1 teaspoon of garlic
- 1 tablespoon of flour
- ¼ cup of dry white wine
- 1 ½ cups of chicken or vegetable broth
- ½ cup of whole milk
- 1 ½ cups of potatoes, cut into small (1/3-inch) cubes
- 1 cup of frozen corn kernels
- 2 teaspoon of diced canned chipotle peppers in adobo sauce
- ¾ teaspoon of salt
- ½ teaspoon of ground black pepper
- ½ teaspoon of dried thyme
- ½ pound of shrimp, peeled and deveined
- ¼ cup of heavy cream

Cooking Instructions:

1. Press the 'Sauté' button on your Instant Pot and add the bacon.
2. Coo the bacon until crisp, for about 3 minutes, stirring frequently. Add the onions, celery and garlic.
3. Cook for about 3 minutes or until the veggies have softened. Stir in flour and sauté for additional 1 minute.
4. Select the 'Cancel' button and deglaze the pot with white wine to remove any browned bits stuck to the pot.
5. Add 1 tbsp. of broth if not completely deglazed. Stir in broth, milk, potatoes, corn, Chipotle, salt, black pepper and thyme.
6. Close and lock the lid in place. Select Manual, High Pressure for 1 minute. When the timer beeps, do a quick pressure release.
7. Carefully open the lid and stir in shrimp and cream. Close and lock the lid in place to cook the shrimp in the residual heat for about 10 minutes.
8. Garnish with scallions, parsley and/or crumbled bacon and serve immediately.

Cajun Shrimp and Sausage Boil

Preparation time: 10 minutes

Cook time: 10 minutes

Total time: 20 minutes

Yield: 4

Ingredients:

- ½ lb. of smoked sausage, cut into four pieces
- 4 ears corn
- 2 red potatoes, cut in half
- 1 tbsp. of Louisiana Shrimp and Crab Boil
- Enough water to cover

To Add to Pot Later:

- ½ lb. of raw shrimp

For Sauce:

- 6 tbsp. of butter
- 1 tbsp. of garlic, minced
- 1/8 tsp. of Cajun seasoning
- ¼ tsp. of Old Bay seasoning
- 3-5 shakes hot sauce, such as Louisiana Hot sauce or Tabasco
- 1/8 tsp. of lemon pepper
- ½ lemon, juiced

Cooking Instructions:

1. Add the sausage, corn, and potatoes into the bottom of your Instant Pot and pour enough water to cover.
2. Add in the Louisiana Shrimp and Crab Boil Mix. Close and lock the lid in place. Select Manual, High Pressure for 4 minutes.
3. Meanwhile in a pan over medium-high heat, melt the better. Add the minced garlic and sauté, stirring frequently to boil the butter and have the garlic flavor.
4. Add all the remaining spices and give everything a good mix. When the timer beeps, do a quick pressure release.
5. Carefully remove the lid and check the potatoes for doneness. The potatoes should be very tender, but not mushy.

6. Add the shrimp and stir well. Once the shrimp turns pink, remove them out, and then remove out the corn, potatoes, and sausage.
7. Add everything bit by bit into the sauce, stirring constantly to coat everything with the spiced butter goodness, starting with the shrimp to cook just a little more.
8. Serve immediately and enjoy!

Lemon Pepper Salmon

Preparation time: 5 minutes

Cook time: 10 minutes

Total time: 15 minutes

Yield: 3 - 4

Ingredients:

- ¾ cup of water
- A few sprigs of parsley dill, tarragon, basil or a combo
- 1 lb. of salmon filet skin on
- 3 tsp. of ghee or other healthy fat divided
- ¼ tsp. of salt
- ½ tsp. of pepper
- ½ lemon, thinly sliced
- 1 zucchini, julienned
- 1 red bell pepper, julienned
- 1 carrot, julienned

Cooking Instructions:

1. Pour the water into the bottom of your Instant Pot and add the herbs.
2. Place the steamer rack and ensure that the handles are extended up. Place salmon, skin down on rack.
3. Drizzle the salmon with ghee/fat, season with salt and pepper, and cover with lemon slices.
4. Close and lock the lid in place and ensure that the valve is in sealing position. Select the Steam button to cook for 3 minutes. While the salmon cooks, julienne your veggies.
5. When the timer beeps, do a quick pressure release. Carefully open the lid and remove rack with salmon and transfer on a bowl. Remove herbs and discard.
6. Add the veggies into the Instant Pot. Close and lock the lid in place. Select the "Sauté" button and allow the veggies cook for about 1 or 2 minutes.
7. Add the remaining teaspoon of fat to the pot and pour a little of the sauce over them if desired.
8. Serve veggies with salmon and enjoy!

Lobster Bisque

Preparation time: 10 minutes

Cook time: 4 minutes

Total time: 14 minutes

Ingredients:

- 1 cup of diced carrots
- 1 cup of diced celery
- 29 ounces canned petite diced tomatoes
- 2 whole shallots, minced
- 1 clove garlic, minced
- 1 tablespoon of butter
- 32 ounces low-sodium chicken broth
- 1 tablespoon of Old Bay Seasoning
- 1 teaspoon of dried dill
- 1 teaspoon of freshly ground black pepper
- ½ teaspoon of paprika
- 4 lobster tails (or 24 ounces frozen lobster)
- 1 pint heavy whipping cream

Cooking Instructions:

1. In a microwave safe bowl, add the butter, minced shallots and garlic.
2. Microwave on high for about 2-3 minutes, or until shallots and garlic are translucent. Add the tomatoes, carrots, celery, minced shallots and garlic into your Instant Pot.
3. Add the chicken broth and spices. If you desire full lobster tails, cut off the fan at the end of the lobster with a knife. Otherwise add the frozen lobster into the Instant Pot.
4. Close and lock the lid in place. Select Manual, High Pressure for 4 minutes. When the timer beeps, do a natural pressure release.
5. Carefully open the lid and if you used lobster tails, remove them from your Instant Pot and peel the flesh from the tails.
6. Puree the soup mixture to your desired chunkiness with an immersion blender. Add the cream and give everything a good stir.
7. Serve and enjoy!

Cioppino Seafood Stew

Preparation time: 10 minutes

Cook time: 10 minutes

Total time: 30 minutes

Yield: 6

Ingredients:

For the Stew Base:

- ¼ cup of vegetable oil
- 14.5 oz. canned fire-roasted tomatoes
- 1 cup of diced onion
- 1 cup of chopped carrots or 1 cup of chopped bell pepper
- 1 cup of water
- 1 cup of white wine or broth
- 2 bay leaves
- 1 tbsp. of tomato paste
- 2 tbsp. of minced garlic
- 2 tsp. of fennel seeds, toasted and ground
- 1 tsp. of dried oregano
- 2 tsp. of salt
- 1 tsp. of red pepper flakes

For Finishing:

- 4 cups of mixed seafood such as fish chunks, shrimp, bay scallops, mussels and calamari rings
- 1-2 tbsp. of fresh lemon juice
- Toasted, crusty bread, for serving

Cooking Instructions:

1. For the stew base: Add the oil, tomato, onions, carrots or bell pepper into the bottom of your Instant Pot.
2. Pour the water and add the wine, bay leaves, tomato paste, garlic, oregano, ground fennel seeds, salt and pepper. Give everything a good stir.
3. Close and lock the lid in place and ensure that the valve is in sealing position. Select Manual, High Pressure for 15 minutes.
4. When the timer beeps, do a natural pressure release for 10 minutes, then quick release any remaining pressure.

5. Carefully open the lid. Select the Sauté button and add the fish, mussels, bay scallops, and calamari rings to the pot.
6. Bring the pot to a boil and add in the shrimp. Cook the contents until all the seafood is cooked through. Add lemon juice right before serving.
7. Serve with crusty bread and enjoy!

INSTANT POT POULTRY RECIPES

Teriyaki Chicken and Rice

Preparation time: 5 minutes

Cook time: 23 minutes

Total time: 43 minutes

Servings: 4

Ingredients:

- 2 cups of low sodium chicken broth
- 1/3 cup of low sodium soy sauce
- ¼ cup of hoisin sauce
- 1 tbsp. of white vinegar
- 1 tbsp. of liquid honey
- 2 tsp. of minced garlic
- 1 tsp. of minced ginger
- 1 pinch red pepper flakes, optional
- 1 ½ cups of long grain brown rice
- 2 boneless skinless chicken breasts
- 1 red bell pepper, chopped
- 1 large carrot, finely diced
- 1 cup of frozen peas

Cooking Instructions:

1. Add the broth, soy sauce, hoisin sauce, vinegar, honey, garlic, ginger and pepper flakes if desired into the bottom of your Instant Pot.
2. Give everything a good stir. Stir in the rice and add the chicken breasts on top.
3. Close and lock the lid in place and ensure that the valve is in sealing position.
4. Select Manual, High Pressure for 20 minutes. When the timer beeps, perform a quick pressure release.
5. Carefully open the lid in place and add give everything a good stir.
6. Serve immediately and enjoy!

Salsa Lime Chicken

Preparation time: 5 minutes

Cook time: 25 minutes

Total time: 30 minutes

Servings: 6

Ingredients:

- 3 chicken breasts
- 16 oz. of Salsa
- Juice from 1 lime

Cooking Instructions:

1. Add the chicken breasts into the bottom of your Instant Pot.
2. Pour the salsa over the chicken in your pot. Pour lime juice over the top of the salsa.
3. Close and lock the lid in place and ensure that the valve is in sealing position.
4. Select Poultry button to cook for 25 minutes. When the timer beeps, perform a quick pressure release.
5. Carefully open the lid and give everything a good stir.
6. Serve and enjoy!

Chicken Adobo

Serves 4 - 6

Preparation time: 5 minutes

Cook time: 30 minutes

Total time: 35 minutes

Ingredients:

- 10 chicken drumsticks
- Kosher salt
- 2 tbsp. of avocado oil (or canola oil)
- ½ yellow onion, sliced
- 10 - 12 garlic gloves, peeled and chopped
- ½ cup of soy sauce
- ½ cup of distilled white vinegar (apple cider vinegar is will work too)
- ¼ cup of water
- 3 bay leaves
- 1 ½ tsp. of ground black pepper

Cooking Instructions:

1. Generously season the chicken drumsticks with salt and pepper.
2. Press the Sauté function on your Instant Pot and oil. Add the chicken pieces, and sauté in batches if necessary, until browned on all sides.
3. Add all the chicken to the pot. Add in rest of the ingredients. Close and lock the lid in place and ensure that the valve is in sealing position.
4. Select Manual, High Pressure for 9 minutes. When the timer beeps, do a natural pressure release for about 10 minutes.
5. Carefully remove the lid and discard the bay leaves. Press the Sauté function and simmer for about 10 - 15 minutes or until sauce thickens slightly.
6. Transfer chicken to a serving bowl and top with sauce.
7. Serve with rice and enjoy!

Turkey Breast

Preparation time: 5 minutes

Cook time: 35 minutes

Total time: 40 minutes

Servings: 6

Ingredients:

- 5-6 pounds of bone-in, skin-on turkey breast
- Sea salt to taste
- Black pepper to taste
- 1 ½ cup of chicken broth
- 1 yellow onion, sliced
- 1 garlic head, sliced across cloves
- 8 thyme sprigs
- 1 rosemary sprig
- 1 lemon, sliced

Cooking Instructions:

1. Defrost the turkey breast and season with salt and pepper.
2. Add rest of the ingredients to pot – chicken broth, onions, garlic, thyme, rosemary. Add the trivet on top of all ingredients into the bottom of your Instant Pot.
3. Add the turkey breast on top of trivet, skin side up. Close and lock in place and ensure that the valve is in sealing.
4. Select Manual, High Pressure for 35 minutes. When the time is up, do a natural pressure release for about 15 minutes.
5. Carefully open the lid and transfer the turkey breast to a baking tray with tongs. Broil with your broiler until the skin reaches desired crispiness.
6. Serve and enjoy!

Honey Garlic Chicken

Preparation time: 5 minutes

Cook time: 20 minutes

Total time: 25 minutes

Servings: 4

Ingredients:

- 1/3 cup of honey
- 4 cloves garlic, minced
- ½ cup of low sodium soy sauce
- ½ cup no salt ketchup
- ½ tsp. of dried oregano
- 2 tbsp. of chopped fresh parsley
- 1 tbsp. of sesame seed oil
- 4 - 6 bone-in, skinless chicken thighs
- Kosher salt
- Fresh ground pepper, to taste
- ½ tbsp. of toasted sesame seeds, for garnish
- Sliced green onions, for garnish

Cooking Instructions:

1. In a medium bowl, combine together the honey, minced garlic, soy sauce, ketchup, oregano and parsley.
2. Give everything a good mix until well combined and set aside. Press the Sauté function on your Instant Pot and add the oil.
3. Generously season the chicken thighs with salt and pepper. Carefully arrange the chicken thighs in the instant pot and cook for about 2 to 3 minutes on each side.
4. Add the prepared honey garlic sauce to the pot. Close and lock the lid in place and ensure that the valve is in sealing position.
5. Select the Poultry button to cook for 20 minutes. When the timer beeps, do a quick pressure release. Carefully open the lid and remove the chicken to a serving bowl.
6. Spoon the sauce over the chicken. Garnish with toasted sesame seeds and green onions.
7. Serve and enjoy!

Mongolian Chicken

Preparation time: 10 minutes

Cook time: 20 minutes

Total time: 40 minutes

Ingredients:

- 4 boneless skinless chicken breasts cut into 1 – 2 inch cubes
- 2 tbsp. of extra virgin olive oil
- ¾ cup of brown sugar
- 4 garlic cloves, minced
- 1 tbsp. of fresh ginger, minced
- ¾ cup of lite soy sauce (use ½ cup if you are sensitive to sodium)
- ¾ cup of water or chicken broth
- 1 cup of carrots, chopped
- 1 tsp. of red pepper flakes
- 1 tbsp. of garlic powder

Cornstarch Slurry:

- 2 tbsp. of cornstarch

Optional:

- ¼ cup green onions, chopped
- 1 tsp. of sesame seeds

Rice (optional):

- 2 cups of basmati rice
- 2 cups of water
- 2 tbsp. of herbed or unsalted butter
- ¼ tsp. of salt

Cooking Instructions:

1. Press the Sauté button on your Instant Pot and add the oil.
2. Add the chicken and cook for about 2-3 minutes, stirring a couple of times. Sauté until the chicken begins to turn golden.
3. Deglaze the pot with ¼ cup of water using a wooden spoon to scrape any browned bits stuck to the bottom of the pot.

4. Add the minced garlic, minced ginger, lite soy sauce, brown sugar, water, carrots, garlic powder and red pepper flakes.
5. Give everything a good stir until all the ingredients are combined and coated in sauce.
6. Serve and enjoy!

Creamy Italian Chicken Breasts

Preparation time: 10 minutes

Cook time: 8 minutes

Total time: 18 minutes

Servings: 4

Ingredients:

- 8 boneless skinless chicken breasts
- 1 cup of low sodium chicken broth
- 1 tsp. of minced garlic
- 1 tsp. of Italian seasoning
- ¼ tsp. of salt
- ¼ tsp. of black pepper
- 1/3 cup of heavy cream
- 1/3 cup of roasted red peppers
- 1 ½ tbsp. of corn starch
- 1 tbsp. of basil pesto

Cooking Instructions:

1. Add the chicken breasts into the bottom of your Instant Pot.
2. Add the broth and sprinkle with garlic, Italian seasoning, salt and pepper. Close and lock the lid in place and ensure that the valve is in sealing position.
3. Select Manual, High Pressure for 8 minutes. When the timer beeps, do a natural pressure release for about 5 minutes, then quick release any remaining pressure.
4. Carefully open the lid and transfer the chicken breasts to a cutting board. Shred the chicken with two forks.
5. Press the Sauté function. Stir in cream, red peppers, corn starch and pesto into the pot. Give everything a good whisk and sauté for about 4 minutes, until thickened.
6. Return the chicken back to the sauce and give everything a good stir. Serve with the sauce over top if desired.

Chicken Marsala

Preparation time: 5 minutes

Cook time: 15 minutes

Total time: 20 minutes

Yield: 4

Ingredients:

- 2 tablespoons of butter
- Flour for dredging
- 1 - 1.5 lb. of thinly sliced chicken breasts
- 8-12 oz. sliced mushrooms
- 4 oz. of pancetta, finely cubed
- 2/3 cup of marsala cooking wine
- 1 cup of chicken broth
- 2 cloves garlic, minced
- 1 tablespoon cornstarch + 1 tablespoon of water
- Fresh parsley, to garnish

Cooking Instructions:

1. Press the sauté button on your Instant Pot and add butter to melt. Dredge the chicken breasts in flour on both sides and add into the bottom of your Instant Pot.
2. Allow the chicken breasts to brown in the butter for 1-2 minutes on each side, then remove and set aside. Add the garlic, pancetta, mushrooms and Marsala wine and cook for about 2 minutes.
3. Press the Cancel function. Add the chicken breasts into the Instant Pot together with chicken broth, nestling chicken down into the mushrooms. Close and lock the lid in place.
4. Select Manual, High Pressure for 15 minutes. When the timer beeps, do a quick pressure release. Carefully open the lid and take out the chicken breasts from the pot.
5. Press the Sauté function and wait to bubble for 1 minute until sauce begins to bubble. Add the mixture of cornstarch and water and allow to simmer for about 5 to 10 minutes, stirring occasionally while sauce thickens.
6. Add the chicken on bowls, spoon mushroom sauce over chicken, garnish with parsley and serve immediately.

Chicken Cordon Bleu

Preparation time: 12 minutes

Cook time: 15 minutes

Total time: 27 minutes

Servings: 4

Ingredients:

- 2 cup of panko breadcrumbs
- 1 teaspoon of salt
- ½ teaspoon of pepper
- 3-4 chicken breast halves boneless, skinless
- 8 slices deli ham, thinly sliced
- 4 slices Swiss cheese
- ½ cup of butter, melted
- 1 cup of chicken broth

Cooking Instructions:

1. In a medium bowl, combine together the panko, salt, and pepper and set aside.
2. Pound the chicken breast to 1/2" thickness to break through the meat. Add 2 slices of ham over each chicken breast.
3. Add slice of Swiss cheese over the ham and roll up the chicken. Carefully dip the chicken rolls in butter, then roll in breadcrumbs.
4. Add the dipped chicken rolls into the bottom of your Instant Pot. Pour the rest of the butter over the chicken. Pour the chicken broth in the cracks between the chicken breasts.
5. Close and lock the lid in place and ensure that the valve is in sealing position. Select Manual, High Pressure for 8 minutes.
6. When the timer beeps, do a natural pressure release for about 5 minutes, then quick release any remaining pressure.
7. Carefully open the lid and transfer the chicken to a cutting board. Shred the chicken with two forks and return back to the pot. Give everything a good stir.
8. Serve and enjoy!

Chicken Chile Verde

Yield: 6

Preparation time: 5 minutes

Cook time: 25 minutes

Total time: 30 minutes

Ingredients:

- 2 pounds of chicken thighs or chicken breasts
- ½ tsp. of ground cumin
- ¼ tsp. of garlic powder
- 16 oz. salsa verde
- Kosher salt to taste
- Black pepper, to taste

Cooking Instructions:

1. Add the chicken into the bottom of your Instant Pot.
2. Add the cumin, garlic powder, and salsa verde. Close and lock the lid in place and ensure that the valve is in sealing position.
3. Select Manual, High Pressure for 25 minutes. When the timer beeps, do a quick pressure release.
4. Carefully open the lid and shred the chicken with two forks. Season with salt and black pepper, to taste.
5. Serve with tortillas, rice, use in burritos, quesadillas, tacos, salads if desired and enjoy.

INSTANT POT BEAN & GRAIN RECIPES

Refried Black Beans

Servings: 5 cups

Preparation time: 10 minutes

Total time: 22 minutes

Cook time: 32 minutes

Ingredients:

- 1 pound of dried black beans (about 2 cups)
- 1 white onion, peeled, halved
- 2 tablespoons of lard or vegetable oil
- 1 ½ teaspoon of kosher salt
- 1 sprig cilantro, for serving
- Grated cotija cheese, chopped radishes, and lime wedges, for serving

Cooking Instructions:

1. Combine together the beans, onion, lard, salt, cilantro sprig, and 6 cups water into the bottom of your Instant Pot.
2. Close and lock the lid in place and ensure that the valve is in sealing position. Select Manual, High Pressure for 22 minutes.
3. When the timer beeps, do a natural pressure release for about 15 minutes. Carefully open the lid and give everything a good stir.
4. Press the "Sauté" button. Simmer and mash beans with a potato masher or large wooden spoon against the pot.
5. Continue to cook, stirring occasionally for about 5 minutes or until the liquid thickens. Adjust the seasoning with more salt to taste.
6. Divide beans among plates and top with cheese, cilantro, radishes, and limes. Serve immediately and enjoy!

Spiced Coconut Chicken and Rice

Serves: 4 – 5

Preparation time: 10 minutes

Cook time: 17 minutes

Total time: 27 minutes

Ingredients:

- 1 tbsp. of extra-virgin olive oil
- 1 onion, cut into 1/4-inch slices
- 1 (1-inch) piece ginger, peeled and cut into 1/4-inch slices
- 3 medium garlic cloves, minced
- 1 tbsp. of curry powder
- 1 tsp. of ground turmeric
- 2 lb. of bone-in, skin-on chicken thighs
- Kosher salt
- Freshly ground black pepper
- 1 (14 oz.) can light coconut milk
- ½ cup of water
- 1 1/3 cups of jasmine rice, rinsed
- 2 tbsp. of cilantro leaves plus stems, stems and leaves divided
- 1 ½ tsp. of sugar
- 1 lime, halved (one half cut into wedges, for serving)

Cooking Instructions:

1. Press the Sauté on high heat on your Instant Pot and add the oil. When hot, add the onion and ginger and cook for about 2 minutes.
2. Add the garlic, curry powder, and turmeric and sauté for additional 1 minute. Add the chicken and season with salt and pepper. Pour the coconut milk and water.
3. Close and lock the lid in place and ensure that the valve is in sealing position. Select Manual, High Pressure for 13 minutes.
4. When the timer beeps, do a quick pressure release. Carefully open the lid and remove the chicken to a bowl.
5. Add the rice, chopped cilantro stems, and sugar. Close and lock the lid in place. Select Manual, High Pressure for 4 minutes.
6. Remove the skin and bones from the chicken and discard. When the rice is cooked, press the Cancel button.

7. Do a natural pressure release for about 10 minutes, then quick release any remaining pressure.
8. Return the chicken back to your Instant Pot and pour the juice of half the lime. Give everything a good stir and season with salt and pepper.
9. Serve in bowls topped with cilantro leaves and lime wedges.

Mexican Rice and Beans

Preparation time: 5 minutes

Cook time: 35 minutes

Total time 1 hour

Servings: 8

Calories: 285 kcal

Ingredients:

- ½ tbsp. of avocado oil
- 1 onion, diced
- 1 yellow or red pepper, diced
- 1 tsp. of minced garlic
- 2 cups of short grain brown rice
- 1 cup of dried red beans
- 1 cup of salsa
- 1 tbsp. of taco seasoning
- 5 cups of vegetable or chicken stock
- Cheese, sour cream, cilantro for serving

Cooking Instructions:

1. Press the Sauté button on high and add the oil.
2. Add the onions, and peppers and cook for about 2-3 minutes until just it starts to soften up. Add in garlic and cook for additional 1 minute.
3. Add in rice, beans, salsa, seasonings and stock, and give everything a good stir. Close and lock the lid in place and ensure that the valve is in sealing position.
4. Press the Cancel button. Select Manual, High Pressure for 35 minutes. When the timer beeps, do a natural press release.
5. Carefully remove the lid and give everything a good stir.
6. Serve with desired toppings and enjoy!

New Orleans-Style Red Beans and Rice

Servings: 6 - 8

Preparation time: 10 minutes

Cook time: 50 minutes

Total time: 1 hour

Ingredients:

- 1 tbsp. of oil
- 1 lb. of smoked sausage, sliced
- ¼ stick of butter
- 2 cups of chopped seasoning blend (onions, celery, green bell peppers, parsley flakes)
- 1 clove garlic, chopped
- 1 (1 lb.) package Camellia Brand Red Kidney Beans
- 6 cups of water
- 1 bay leaf
- Salt to taste
- Pepper to taste
- Cajun seasoning to taste
- Hot cooked rice

Cooking Instructions:

1. Rinse and sort the beans. Select the Sauté function on your Instant Pot, and add oil. Once hot, add the sliced sausage, and cook for about 5 minutes or until browned.
2. Remove the sausage to a paper towel-lined plate and set aside. Add ¼ stick butter to the Instant Pot, along with the chopped seasoning blend and garlic, and sauté the ingredients until onions has softened.
3. Return the cooked sausage to pot, along with the beans, water, and bay leaf and give everything a good stir. Press the Cancel function.
4. Close and lock the lid in place. Select Manual, High Pressure for 40 minutes. When the time is up, do a natural pressure release for about 20 minutes.
5. Carefully open the lid and use a potato masher or spoon to mash beans to your desired creamy consistency. Add the salt, pepper, and Cajun seasoning to taste.
6. Serve warm over cooked rice and enjoy!

Pinto Beans & Ham Hocks

Servings: 6

Preparation time: 10 minutes

Cook time: 40 minutes

Total time: 50 minutes

Ingredients:

- 1 (1 lb.) package Camellia Brand Pinto Beans
- 1 large smoked ham hock
- 1 medium yellow onion, chopped
- 2 large cloves garlic, minced
- 2 dried red chili peppers, or ¼ tsp. of red chili flakes
- ¾ tsp. of salt
- ¼ tsp. of freshly ground black pepper
- 6 cups of water or chicken broth
- 1 bunch green onions, chopped

Cooking Instructions:

1. Rinse and sort the beans. Add the beans and ham hock into the bottom of your Instant Pot with onion, chilies, salt, pepper, and water or broth.
2. Close and lock the lid in place and ensure that the valve is in sealing position. Select Manual, High Pressure for 40 minutes.
3. When the timer beeps, do a natural pressure release for about 20 minutes. Carefully open the lid and remove the ham hocks with tongs.
4. Discard the skin, bones and cartilage. Chop or shred ham and return back into beans. Mash some of the beans with a potato masher to make the creamier.
5. Serve sprinkled with green onions and enjoy.

Chicken Tinga & Black Bean Tacos

Preparation time: 5 minutes

Cook time: 20 minutes

Total time: 25 minutes

Yield: 8 tacos

Ingredients:

- 1 (14 oz.) can whole tomatoes
- ½ cup of jarred salsa verde
- 1-2 tbsp. of Tabasco chipotle pepper sauce
- ¼ - ½ onion, chopped
- 3 garlic cloves, chopped
- ½ tsp. of cumin
- ½ tsp. of dried oregano
- A dash of salt
- 2 lb. of chicken tenderloins
- Pepper to taste
- 1 bay leaf
- Cooked Instant Pot Camellia Brand Black Beans
- Small corn or flour tortillas
- Chopped white onion
- Chopped fresh cilantro
- Chopped radishes
- Lime wedges

Cooking Instructions:

1. Blend the first 8 ingredients until the mixture is smooth with a blender or food processor.
2. Add the chicken into the bottom of your Instant Pot, season with salt and pepper, and pour tomato mixture over chicken.
3. Add the bay leaf and give everything a good stir to combine. Close and lock the lid in place and ensure that the valve is in sealing position.
4. Select Manual, High Pressure for 10 minutes. When the timer beeps, do a natural pressure release for about 5 minutes, then quick release any remaining pressure.
5. Carefully remove the lid and discard the bay leaf. Remove the chicken to a cutting board and shred with two forks.
6. Meanwhile, warm the tortillas while the chicken is cooking in the Instant Pot by wrapping in aluminum foil and heating in a 350° oven for about 15 - 20 minutes.

7. Return the shredded chicken back to the pot and cooked black beans to warm tortillas, along with more chopped onion, cilantro, radishes and fresh squeezed lime juice.
8. Give everything a good stir.
9. Serve and enjoy!

Mexican Pinto Beans

Preparation time: 5 minutes

Cook time: 75 minutes

Total time: 80 minutes

Yield: 8 cups

Ingredients:

- 2 lb. of dry pinto beans
- 1 white or yellow onion, halved
- 2 garlic cloves
- 1 tsp. of salt
- 8 cups of water
- 1 bay leaf, optional
- 2 sprigs cilantro, optional
- 1 fresh jalapeño, optional

Cooking Instructions:

1. Add all ingredients into the bottom of your Instant Pot.
2. Close and lock the lid in place and ensure that the valve is in sealing position.
3. Select Manual, High Pressure for 35 minutes.
4. When the timer beeps, do a natural pressure release for about 20 minutes. Carefully open the lid and remove the aromatics.
5. Generously season with additional salt to taste if desired. Give everything a good stir.
6. Serve and enjoy!

Cherry & Spice Rice Pudding

Preparation time: 10 minutes

Cook time: 3 minutes

Total time: 13 minutes

Ingredients:

- 4 cups of cooked rice
- 1 can (12 oz.) evaporated milk
- 1 cup 2% milk
- 1/3 cup of sugar
- ¼ cup of water
- ¾ cup of dried cherries
- 3 tbsp. of butter, softened
- 2 tsp. of vanilla extract
- ½ tsp. of ground cinnamon
- ¼ tsp. of ground nutmeg

Cooking Instructions:

1. Generously grease your Instant Pot and add the rice.
2. Add the milks, sugar and water and give everything a good stir to combine. Stir in the rest of the ingredients.
3. Close and lock the lid in place and ensure that the valve is in sealing position. Select Manual, High Pressure for 3 minutes.
4. When the timer beeps, do a natural pressure release for about 5 minutes, then quick release any remaining pressure.
5. Carefully open the lid and stir lightly.
6. Serve warm or cold. Refrigerate leftovers.

INSTANT POT LAMB, BEEF & PORK RECIPES

Beef and Butternut Squash Stew

Preparation time: 15 minutes

Cook time: 30 minutes

Total time: 45 minutes

Yield: 10

Ingredients:

- 1 medium onion, chopped
- 2 cloves garlic, minced
- 2 celery stalks, chopped
- 2 carrots, chopped
- 2 tablespoons of tomato paste
- 1 tomato, peeled and chopped
- 2 pounds of beef stew cut in 1" pieces
- 4 tablespoons of arrowroot starch
- 6 cups of peeled and chopped butternut squash cut in 1" cubes
- ½ cup of Marsala wine
- 2 ½ cup of beef broth
- 3 tablespoons of extra virgin olive oil
- 2 bay leaves
- 1 teaspoon of sweet Hungarian paprika
- 1 teaspoon of thyme
- 1 teaspoon of rosemary

Cooking Instructions:

1. Select the Sauté button on your Instant Pot and add the 1 tablespoon of olive oil.
2. Add the onions, garlic, celery, carrots, tomato and tomato paste to the pot. Generously season with salt and freshly ground black pepper.
3. Give everything a good stir. Season the beef stew with salt, black pepper and 4 tablespoons of arrowroot starch (or cornstarch).
4. Add the beef and butternut squash into the bottom of your Instant Pot. Season butternut squash with salt and freshly ground black pepper.
5. Season the contents in your pot with sweet Hungarian paprika, thyme, rosemary and add 2 bay leaves. Give everything a good stir.

6. Add the wine and beef broth, and the rest of the 2 tablespoons of olive oil. Close and lock the lid in place and ensure that the valve is in sealing position.
7. Select Meat/Stew function to cook for 30 minutes. When the timer beeps, do a quick pressure release.
8. Carefully open the lid and give everything a good stir.
9. Serve and enjoy!

Boneless Pork Chops

Serves: 2

Preparation time: 10 minutes

Cook time: 7 minutes

Total time: 17 minutes

Ingredients:

- 2 pork chops, boneless 1" thick
- 2 tbsp. of brown sugar
- 1 tsp. of salt
- 1 tsp. of black pepper
- 1 tsp. of paprika
- ½ tsp. of onion powder
- 1 tablespoon of butter
- 1 cup of chicken broth
- ½ tbsp. of Worcestershire sauce
- 1 tsp. of Liquid Smoke

Cooking Instructions:

1. In a medium bowl, mix together all the spices and brown sugar. Season both sides of the pork chops with the spices.
2. Press the Sauté button on your Instant Pot and add 1 tbsp. of butter. When hot, add the pork chops and sauté on both sides for about 1-2 minutes each.
3. Remove the pork chops and set aside. Turn of the Instant Pot. Pour 1 cup of chicken broth and deglaze the pot with a wooden spoon to remove any browned meat stuck to the bottom of the pot.
4. Add the Worcestershire sauce and liquid smoke and add pork chops to the pot. Close and lock the lid in place and ensure that the valve is in sealing position.
5. Select Manual, High Pressure for 7 minutes. When the timer beeps, do a natural pressure release for about 12 minutes, then quick release any remaining pressure.
6. Carefully open the lid and remove the pork chops. Allow the pork chops to sit for about 5 minutes before serving.
7. Serve and enjoy!

Sticky Hoisin Baby Back Ribs

Servings: 4

Preparation time: 10 minutes

Cook time: 12 minutes

Total time: 22 minutes

Ingredients:

- 4 pounds of baby back pork ribs (about 2 racks)
- 2 teaspoons of kosher salt
- 1 teaspoon of freshly ground black pepper
- 1/3 cup of hoisin sauce
- 1/3 cup of honey
- 1/3 cup of soy sauce, preferably dark
- 2 tablespoons of Shaoxing rice wine or dry sherry
- 1 tablespoon of finely chopped fresh ginger
- ½ teaspoon of five-spice powder
- Flaky sea salt

Cooking Instructions:

1. First, cut the meat between bones into individual ribs. Generously season the meat with kosher salt and pepper.
2. Allow it to rest at room temperature at least 30 minutes and up to 1 hour. Whisk hoisin, honey, soy sauce, rice wine, ginger, and five-spice powder into the bottom of your Instant Pot.
3. Add the ribs into the sauce to coat. Arrange the ribs in a single layer and place the remaining ribs on top. Close and lock the lid in place and ensure that the valve is in sealing position.
4. Select Manual, High Pressure for 12 minutes. When the timer beeps, do a quick pressure release. Carefully open the lid and check the ribs for doneness by piercing with a sharp knife.
5. Transfer ribs to a bowl. Press the "Sauté" function and allow to simmer until the cooking liquid is reduced by about half for 10–15 minutes. Brush the meat with sauce.
6. Preheat the broiler and broil the ribs until browned and crisp in places for about 5 minutes.
7. Add ribs to the bowl and top with sea salt.
8. Serve with remaining sauce and enjoy!

Japanese Pork Tender Rib Stew

Preparation time: 10 minutes

Cook time: 60 minutes

Total time: 1 hour 10 minutes

Servings: 2 - 3

Ingredients:

- 820 gm soft pork ribs (pork cartilage)
- 4 slices ginger
- 1 clove garlic, minced
- 3 tablespoons of (60 ml) Japanese salt-reduced light soy sauce
- 2 tablespoons of (40 ml) mirin
- 1 tablespoon of (20 ml) cooking rice wine
- 3 teaspoons of white vinegar
- ½ tablespoon of (10 gm) rock sugar, roughly pounded
- 1 cup of water
- 400 gm radish, peeled and roughly chopped
- Salt, to taste
- Spring onion, for garnish

Thickening:

- 2 teaspoons of corn flour / corn starch
- 1 tablespoon of water

Cooking Instructions:

1. Blanch the pork ribs for a couple of minutes, drain well and set aside. Select the Sauté function on your Instant Pot and add the oil.
2. Sauté the pork ribs to brown on both sides working in batches. Add all the pork ribs into the pot. Add in ginger, garlic, soy sauce, mirin, wine, vinegar, rock sugar and water.
3. Close and lock the lid in place and ensure that the valve is in sealing position. Select "Meat/Stew" button to cook for 35 minutes. When the timer beeps, do a quick pressure release.
4. Carefully open the lid and add in the radish. Close and lock the lid in place. Select "Meat/Stew" button for additional 10 minutes.
5. When the timer beeps, do a quick pressure release. Carefully remove the lid and stir. Select the "Sauté" function to reduce the cooking liquid by half.

6. Adjust the seasoning with salt. Stir in the thickening and cook until your desired consistency is achieved. Garnish with spring onion.
7. Serve warm and enjoy!

Cuban Pulled Pork Sandwiches

Preparation time: 10 minutes

Cook: 25 minutes

Total time: 35 minutes

Servings: 16

Ingredients:

- 1 boneless pork shoulder butt roast (4 - 5 lb.)
- 2 tsp. of salt
- 2 tsp. of pepper
- 1 tbsp. of olive oil
- 1 cup of orange juice
- ½ cup of lime juice
- 12 garlic cloves, minced
- 2 tbsp. of spiced rum, optional
- 2 tbsp. of ground coriander
- 2 tsp. of white pepper
- 1 tsp. of cayenne pepper

Sandwiches:

- 2 loaves (1 lb.) French bread
- Yellow mustard, optional
- 16 dill pickle slices
- 1 - ½ lb. of thinly sliced deli ham
- 1 - ½ lb. of Swiss cheese, sliced

Cooking Instructions:

1. First, cut the pork into 2-inch thick pieces and generously season with salt and pepper.
2. Press the Sauté button on your Instant Pot and add the oil. Sauté the pork to brown on each sides working in batches. Transfer the pork to a bowl.
3. Add the orange and lime juices, and deglaze the pot by scrapping to remove any browned bits from bottom of cooker.
4. Add the garlic, rum, if desired, coriander, white pepper and cayenne pepper. Add the pork back into the pot along with the juices.
5. Close and lock the lid in place and ensure that the valve is in sealing position. Select Manual, High Pressure for 25 minutes.

6. When the timer beeps, do a natural pressure release for about 10 minutes, then quick release any remaining pressure.
7. Carefully open the lid and remove roast to a bowl. Shred the roast with two forks. Remove 1 cup of cooking liquid from the pot and pour over the pork and toss to combine.
8. Cut each loaf of bread in half lengthwise. Spread mustard over cut sides of bread if desired. Layer bottom halves of bread with pickles, pork, ham and cheese.
9. Serve and enjoy!

Pork Vindaloo

Servings: 6

Preparation time: 10 minutes

Cook time: 25 minutes

Total time: 35 minutes

Ingredients:

- 3 lb. (1.44 kg) boneless pork shoulder, cubed
- 1 tsp. of sea salt
- ¼ cup of olive oil
- 1 large white onion, peeled and finely chopped
- 4 cloves garlic, peeled and minced
- 1 piece fresh ginger, peeled and grated
- 2 tbsp. of vindaloo seasoning or Madras curry
- 1 tsp. of hot paprika
- ½ tsp. of ground turmeric
- 3 tbsp. of all-purpose flour
- 1/3 cup (80 ml) of Champagne vinegar
- 1 (14 ½ oz.) can diced tomatoes in juice, undrained
- 1 cup (250 ml) reduced-sodium chicken broth

Cooking Instructions:

1. Season the pork with a salt. Press the Sauté button on your Instant Pot and add 2 tbsp. olive oil.
2. Working in a batches, sauté the meat in a single layer on both sides, for about 5 to 7 minutes per batch.
3. Transfer the browned pork with a slotted spoon to a bowl. Add the chopped white onion and sauté, stirring for about 3 minutes, or until soft.
4. Stir in garlic, ginger, and spices. Cook, stirring, for additional 30 seconds. Sprinkle in all-purpose flour and give everything a good stir.
5. Add the browned pork to your Instant Pot. Stir in vinegar, tomatoes with their juice and chicken broth. Deglaze the pot, scrapping to remove any browned bits from the bottom of the pot.
6. Bring the pot to a boil. Close and lock the lid in place and ensure that the valve is in sealing position.
7. Select Manual, High Pressure for 25 minutes. When the timer beeps, do a natural pressure release for about 15 minutes.
8. Carefully remove the lid skim any fat from the top of sauce. Sprinkle with fresh chopped cilantro and serve immediately.

Korean Beef

Preparation time: 15 minutes

Cook time: 40 minutes

Total time: 55 minutes

Yield: 8

Ingredients:

- ½ cup of reduced-sodium soy sauce
- 1/3 cup of brown sugar packed
- ¼ cup of reduced-sodium beef broth
- 5 cloves garlic, minced
- 2 tbsp. of sesame oil
- 2 tbsp. of rice vinegar
- 2 tbsp. of freshly grated ginger
- 2-4 tbsp. of Gochujang sauce, depending on desired heat
- ½ tsp. of onion powder
- ½ tsp. of pepper
- 3-4 lb. of boneless beef chuck roast cut into 1-inch cubes

Cooking Instructions:

1. In a small bowl, whisk together the first 10 ingredients.
2. Add the cubed roast into the bottom of your Instant Pot.
3. Pour sauce over cubed meat. Close and lock the lid in place and ensure that the valve is in sealing position.
4. Select the Meat function, and adjust time to 40 minutes. When the timer beeps, do a natural pressure release for about 25 minutes.
5. Carefully remove the lid and give everything a good stir.
6. Serve and enjoy!

Pork Chops

Preparation time: 10 minutes

Cook time: 7 minutes

Total time: 17 minutes

Ingredients:

- 4 bone-in pork chops
- 1 tbsp. of olive oil
- 1 tarte apple, peeled, cored and sliced
- 2 medium shallots, chopped
- 1 tsp. of chopped fresh thyme
- ½ cup (125 ml) dry white wine
- ½ cup (125 ml) reduced-sodium chicken broth
- 1 tbsp. of Dijon mustard
- 1 tbsp. of grainy mustard
- Sea salt to taste
- Freshly ground black pepper, to taste
- 3 tbsp. of crème fraiche (optional)

Cooking Instructions:

1. Generously season the pork chops with salt and black pepper. Press the Sauté function.
2. Sauté the seasoned pork chops to brown on both sides working in batches. Transfer the browned meat to a bowl using tongs.
3. Add the shallots and apples into the bottom of your Instant Pot. Cook, stirring, until lightly browned. Add the thyme, dry white wine and chicken broth.
4. Deglaze the pot to remove any browned bit stuck to the bottom of the pot. Bring the pot to a boil. Add the pork chops back into the pot.
5. Close and lock the lid in place and ensure that the valve is in sealing position. Select Manual, High Pressure for 7 minutes.
6. When the timer beeps, do a quick pressure release. Carefully open the lid and remove the pork chops to a platter using tongs.
7. Cover with a piece of aluminum foil. Select Sauté function and simmer the liquid in the pot for a couple of seconds to thicken.
8. Stir in mustard and crème fraiche (if desired). Press the Cancel function. Remove aluminum foil from pork chops. Pour mustard sauce over.
9. Serve immediately and enjoy!

Lamb Stew

Preparation time: 10 minutes

Cook time: 35 minutes

Total time: 45 minutes

Ingredients:

- 2 pounds of lamb stew meat (or substitute beef or goat), cut into 1" cubes
- 1 acorn squash, peeled, seeded and cubed
- 3 large carrots, sliced
- 1 medium yellow onion, sliced into half moons
- 1 sprig rosemary
- 1 bay leaf
- 6 cloves garlic, sliced
- 3 tablespoons of broth or water
- ¼ - ½ teaspoon of salt

Cooking Instructions:

1. Add all of the ingredients into the bottom of your Instant Pot.
2. Close and lock the lid in place and ensure that the valve is in sealing position.
3. Select Manual, High Pressure for 35 minutes. When the timer beeps, do a natural pressure release.
4. Carefully remove the lid and give everything a good stir.
5. Serve and enjoy!

Hearty Beef Stew

Preparation time: 10 minutes

Cook time: 35 minutes

Total time: 45 minutes

Ingredients:

- 1 pound of stew meat
- 2 Cups of Beef Stock
- 1 medium onion, chopped
- 3 Yukon gold potatoes, chopped
- 1 cup of carrots, chopped
- 1 tablespoon of oil
- Salt and Pepper to taste
- 1 teaspoon of garlic powder
- 1 teaspoon of paprika
- 2 tablespoons of flour
- 1 tablespoon of tomato paste

Cooking Instructions:

1. Select the "Sauté" button and add the oil and stew meat.
2. Cook the stew meat until the meat is no longer pink. Add in your chopped vegetables and give everything a good stir to combine.
3. Add in your broth and seasonings and stir well. Close and lock the lid in place and ensure that the valve is in sealing position.
4. Select the "Stew/Meat" button to cook for 35 minutes. When the timer beeps, do a quick pressure release.
5. Carefully open the lid and ladle out ¼ of your liquid and combine it with your flour to create a slurry.
6. Return the slurry back into your stew and give everything a good stir to combine.
7. Taste and adjust the seasoning with salt and pepper. Serve warm and enjoy!

INSTANT POT EGG RECIPES

Poached Eggs

Preparation time: 5 minutes

Cook time: 2 minutes

Total time: 7 minutes

Servings: 4

Ingredients:

- 4 large eggs
- 1 cup of water

Cooking Instructions:

1. Place the trivet in the bottom of your Instant Pot and add the 1 cup of water.
2. Generously spray each silicone cup with Pam cooking spray or rub with ghee. Beat each egg and add them into the silicone cup. Cover the cup with foil.
3. Place the silicone cups into trivet and add the trivet into the bottom of your Instant Pot. Close and lock the lid in place and ensure that the valve is in sealing position.
4. Select the "Steam" function to cook for 2 minutes. When the time is up, do a quick pressure release.
5. Carefully open the lid and remove the silicone cups. Break the seal between the egg and the cup with a spoon.
6. Serve immediately and enjoy!

Bacon Cheddar Egg Casserole

Preparation time: 10 minutes

Cook time: 22 minutes

Total time: 32 minutes

Yield: 6 servings

Ingredients:

- 6 eggs
- ½ cup of half and half
- ½ teaspoon of salt
- ¼ teaspoon of pepper
- 1 cup of frozen hash browns
- Pepper to taste
- 2 handfuls of spinach
- ½ cup of bacon bits
- 1 cup of grated cheddar cheese

Cooking Instructions:

1. In a medium bowl, whisk together the eggs and the half and half. Season with ½ teaspoon of salt and ¼ teaspoon of and reserve aside.
2. Spray a heat proof container that will fit into your Instant Pot with non-stick cooking spray. Layer the hash browns in the bottom of the bowl.
3. Season the hash browns with salt and pepper. Layer on the spinach, bacon bits and the cheddar. Pour the egg mixture over the top of everything.
4. Add 1 cup of water into the bottom of your Instant Pot and place the trivet. Cover the casserole bowl with a piece of fowl. Place the bowl in the trivet inside the pot.
5. Close and lock the lid in place and ensure that the valve is in sealing position. Select Manual, High Pressure for 22 minutes.
6. When the timer beeps, do a natural pressure release for about 10 minutes, then quick release any remaining pressure.
7. Carefully open the lid and remove the pan. Remove the foil and cut the casserole with a knife.
8. Serve immediately and enjoy!

Eggy Muffins

Preparation time: 10 minutes

Cook time: 5 minutes

Total time: 15 minutes

Servings: 1 eggy muffin

Ingredients:

- 1 egg
- 4 cherry tomatoes, halved
- 1 tbsp. of shredded cheddar cheese
- Pinch of salt
- Black pepper to taste

Cooking Instructions:

1. Generously grease a small ramekin that will fit into your Instant Pot with cooking spray.
2. Beat the egg into the dish. Add the cherry tomatoes, cheese, and salt and pepper to taste.
3. Add 1 cup of water into the bottom of your Instant Pot and place the trivet. Add the ramekin on top of trivet.
4. Close and lock the lid in place and ensure that the valve is in sealing position. Select Manual, High Pressure for 5 minutes.
5. When the timer beeps, do a quick pressure release. Carefully remove the lid and remove the trivet.
6. Serve and enjoy!

Sous Vide Egg Bites

Preparation time: 5 minutes

Cook time: 10 minutes

Total time: 15 minutes

Ingredients:

- 4 eggs
- ½ cups Monterey jack cheese, shredded
- ½ cup of cottage cheese
- 1 green onion, chopped
- ½ roasted red pepper, chopped
- ¼ cup of spinach, chopped

Cooking Instructions:

1. Pour 1 cup of water into the bottom of your Instant Pot and place the trivet.
2. Add the eggs, Monterey jack, and cottage cheese to a blender and process everything until smooth. Add the green onion, red pepper and spinach and give everything a good stir to combine.
3. Divide the egg mixture evenly between the silicone mold and cover with a piece of aluminum foil. Place the covered silicone mold on top of the trivet.
4. Close and lock the lid in place and ensure that the valve is in sealing position. Select the Steam button to cook for 10 minutes.
5. When the timer beeps, do a natural pressure release for about 10 minutes, then quick release any remaining pressure.
6. Carefully open the lid and remove the silicone mold. Let the egg bites to cool for a couple of minutes before serving.
7. Serve and enjoy!

Sriracha and Red Pepper Deviled Eggs

Preparation time: 10 minutes

Total time: 10 minutes

Servings: 12 deviled eggs

Ingredients:

- 6 hard-boiled eggs, peeled
- 1 tbsp. of sour cream
- 1 tbsp. of Sriracha sauce
- 1 tsp. of freshly squeezed lime juice
- ¼ cup of very finely diced red bell pepper
- 1 tsp. of paprika

Cooking Instructions:

1. In a medium bowl, cut the eggs in half and add the yolks. Add the egg whites in another bowl.
2. Add the sour cream, Sriracha sauce and lime juice. Mash the mixture together until the mixture is smooth and creamy.
3. Add in the diced bell pepper and give everything a good stir to combine.
4. Spoon the mixture into the egg whites. Garnish with a sprinkle of paprika over each deviled egg.
5. Serve and enjoy!

Egg Pudding

Yield: 4

Ingredients:

- Liquid caramel
- 6 eggs
- 6 tbsp. of sugar
- 500 milliliters milk

Cooking Instructions:

1. Evenly spread the liquid caramel in a pudding mold with a cover.
2. In a medium bowl, add the eggs, sugar and milk. Mix everything well with an electric mixer.
3. Pour the mixture into mold and seal with foil. Add the pudding mold into bottom of your Instant Pot.
4. Pour enough water to submerge the container in half. Close and lock the lid in place and ensure that the valve is in sealing position.
5. Select Manual, High Pressure for 10 minutes. When the timer beeps, do a natural pressure release for about 15 minutes.
6. Carefully remove the lid and remove the pudding from the pot. Allow to cool for a couple of minutes.
7. Refrigerate and serve cold.

Cheesy Egg Bake

Preparation time: 5 minutes

Cook time: 20 minutes

Total time: 25 minutes

Servings: 4

Ingredients:

- 6 slices bacon, chopped
- 2 cups of frozen hash browns
- 6 eggs
- ¼ cup of milk
- ½ cup of shredded cheddar cheese
- 1 tsp. of kosher salt
- ½ tsp. of pepper
- Optional add-ins: onion, red pepper, spinach, mushrooms, green onions

Cooking Instructions:

1. Roughly chop up the bacon into bite sizes. Press the Sauté button on your Instant Pot.
2. Add the sliced bacon and cook until crispy. Add in any extra veggies that you desire and sauté until tender for about 3 minutes.
3. Add in frozen hash browns and stir for about 2 minutes, or until slightly thawed. Generously grease a heat proof container that will fit into your Instant Pot.
4. In a medium bowl, whisk together the eggs, milk, shredded cheese, and salt. Add the bacon and veggie mixture to the eggs. Pour the egg mixture into your greased, heat proof container.
5. Add 1 ½ cups of water into the bottom of your Instant Pot and place the trivet. Add the heat proof container with egg mixture on top of trivet.
6. Close and lock the lid in place and ensure that the valve is in sealing position. Select Manual, High Pressure for 20 minutes.
7. When the timer beeps, do a quick pressure release. Loosen the edges with a knife and flip onto large bowl.
8. Serve with green onions and extra shredded cheese!

Chinese Savory Steamed Egg

Serves: 2

Preparation time: 5 minutes

Cook time: 10 minutes

Total time: 15 minutes

Ingredients:

- 2 large eggs
- 175 ml 3/4 cup, warm water, about 80°F / 30°C
- ½ teaspoon of salt
- ⅓ teaspoon of sesame oil
- Soy sauce to taste
- Scallions, for garnish

Cooking Instructions:

1. In a medium bowl, beat together the eggs and add the ½ tsp. of salt until the egg is well beaten.
2. Pour the water to about 80°F in microwave (about 45 secs). Slowly pour the water while stirring the egg in one direction.
3. Add the egg mixture through a strainer to discard the foam and make the egg extra smooth. Cover the bowl with a piece of aluminum foil.
4. Pour 2 cups of water into the bottom of your Instant Pot. Ad d the covered bowl on a rack. Close and lock the lid in place.
5. Select the "Steam" button to cook for 5 minutes. When the timer beeps, do a quick pressure release.
6. Serve and enjoy!

Hard Boiled Eggs

Preparation time: 10 minutes

Cook time: 6 minutes

Total time: 16 minutes

Ingredients:

- Eggs
- 1 cup of water

Cooking Instructions:

1. Place the steamer basket into the bottom of your Instant Pot. Pour the 1 cup of water and add the eggs.
2. Close and lock the lid in place and ensure that the valve is in sealing position. Select Manual, High Pressure for 6 minutes.
3. When the time is up, do a natural pressure release for about 6 minutes, then quick release any remaining pressure.
4. Carefully unlock the lid and remove the steamer basket from the Instant Pot. Add the eggs into ice cold water to cool.
5. Serve and enjoy!

Quick Egg Custard

Preparation time: 5 minutes

Cook time: 7 minutes

Total time: 12 minutes

Servings: 6

Ingredients:

- 4 cups of milk 1%, 2% or whole
- 6 large eggs
- ¾ cup of white sugar
- 1 teaspoon of vanilla extract, optional
- Dash of sea salt
- ¼ tsp. of ground cinnamon, optional
- Garnish: Nutmeg freshly grated, Fresh Fruit, Ground Cinnamon

Cooking Instructions:

1. In a small bowl, beat together all the eggs. Add the milk, sugar, salt and vanilla and blend until combined.
2. Add the mixture into a metal safe bowl and cover with a piece of aluminum foil. Pour 1.5 cups of water into the bottom of your Instant Pot.
3. Place the trivet in bottom and add the metal safe bowl top of trivet. Close and lock the lid in place and ensure that the valve is in sealing position.
4. Select Manual, High Pressure for 7 minutes. When the timer beeps, do a natural pressure release for about 10 minutes.
5. Carefully open the lid and transfer to a bowl. Top with a dusting of nutmeg, berries or other fruit, if desired.
6. Serve and enjoy!

French "Baked" Eggs

Preparation time: 5 minutes

Cook time: 8 minutes

Total time: 13 minutes

Ingredients:

- 4 large eggs
- 4 slices of meat, fish or vegetables
- 4 slices of cheese, or shot of cream
- 4 garnish of fresh herbs
- Olive oil

Cooking Instructions:

1. Pour 1 cup of water into the bottom of your Instant Pot and place the trivet.
2. Grease the ramekins with a drop of olive oil in each. Lay a slice of preferred meat, fish or vegetable. Beat an egg and add it into the ramekin.
3. Add the sliced cheese, or cream, if desired. Cover the ramekins with foil. Place the ramekins into the trivet in your Instant Pot.
4. Close and lock the lid in place and ensure that the valve is in sealing position. Set to cook on Low Pressure for 4 minutes.
5. When the timer beeps, do a quick pressure release. Carefully open the lid and remove the ramekins.
6. Serve immediately and enjoy!

Artichoke and Asparagus Deviled Eggs

Preparation time: 10 minutes

Total time: 10 minutes

Servings: 12

Ingredients:

- 6 hard-boiled eggs, peeled
- ¼ cup of steamed asparagus, chopped
- 1 tbsp. of sour cream
- 1 tbsp. of mayonnaise
- 1 tbsp. of fresh parsley, chopped
- 1 tsp. of mustard
- 1 tsp. of freshly squeezed lemon juice
- ¼ cup of very finely diced marinated artichoke hearts
- ¼ tsp. of fine sea salt

Cooking Instructions:

1. In a medium bowl, cut the eggs in half.
2. Add together the asparagus, sour cream, mayonnaise, parsley, mustard and lemon juice. Blend the mixture until smooth with a hand blender.
3. Add in the very finely diced artichoke hearts and give everything a good stir to combine. Season with sea salt to taste.
4. Spoon the mixture into the egg whites. Garnish with very small tips of asparagus, a sprinkling of parsley and, if desired, a bit of fresh lemon zest.
5. Serve and enjoy!

INSTANT POT VEGAN & VEGETARIAN RECIPES

Vegan Cauliflower Queso

Servings: 4 cups

Preparation time: 10 minutes

Cook time: 5 minutes

Total time: 15 minutes

Ingredients:

Instant Pot ingredients:

- 2 cups (214 g) cauliflower florets (about ½ head small cauliflower)
- 1 cup (237 ml) of water
- ¾ cup (96 g) thick-cut carrot coins
- ¼ cup (34 g) raw cashews

Blender Ingredients:

- ¼ cup (24 g) nutritional yeast
- Liquid drained from 1 (10 ounces) can diced tomatoes with green chiles (We like Rotel)
- ½ teaspoon of smoked paprika
- ½ teaspoon of salt
- ¼ teaspoon of chili powder
- ¼ teaspoon of jalapeño powder, optional
- 1/8 teaspoon of mustard powder

Mix-in Ingredients:

- 1 (10 ounces) can diced tomatoes with green chilies, drained (I like Rotel)
- ½ cup (75 g) of chopped bell pepper, optional
- 2 tablespoons (30 g) of minced red onion, optional
- ¼ cup (4 g) of minced cilantro

Cooking Instructions:

1. Add the cauliflower, water, carrots and cashews into the bottom of your Instant Pot. Close and lock the lid in place.
2. Select Manual, High Pressure for 5 minutes, then quick release any remaining pressure. Pour the cooked mixture into a strainer over the sink and drain the extra water.
3. Add the drained mixture into the blender along with the nutritional yeast, liquid drained from the canned tomatoes, smoked paprika, salt, chili powder, jalapeño powder (if desired) and mustard powder into your blender.
4. Blend everything smooth. Scrape out the blender contents into a medium bowl and stir in the tomatoes and green chilies, bell pepper, minced onion and cilantro.
5. Serve and enjoy!

Veggie Chickpea Potato Soup

Preparation time: 10 minutes

Cook time: 5 minutes

Total time 15 minutes

Servings: 3

Calories: 157 kcal

Ingredients:

- ¼ cup of water or broth
- ½ onion, chopped
- 3 cloves of garlic
- ½ cup of chopped tomato
- 1/8 teaspoon of fennel seeds
- ½ teaspoon of onion powder
- ¼ teaspoon of garlic powder
- 1/8 - ¼ teaspoon of cinnamon
- ½ teaspoon of oregano
- ½ teaspoon of thyme or use 1 teaspoon of fresh rosemary
- 1 large potato cubed small (We used Yukon gold or white,)
- ¾ cup of carrots
- ½ cup of other veggies like peppers mushrooms, zucchini, broccoli
- 1.25 cups of cooked chickpeas or 1 15 ounces can chickpeas drained
- ½ - ¾ teaspoon of salt
- 1 cup of water
- 1 cup of non-dairy milk such as coconut milk almond milk or cashew milk
- 2 cups of spinach
- Freshly ground black pepper for garnish , lemon juice (optional)

Cooking Instructions:

1. Press the Sauté button on your Instant Pot and add the broth. Add the onion and garlic and sauté until golden.
2. Deglaze the pot with a tablespoon of water to remove any browned bits stuck to the bottom of the pot. Add the chopped tomato and give everything a good mix.
3. Add the spices and herbs and mix in. Add the veggies, chickpeas, salt, non-dairy milk and water and give everything a good mix.
4. Close and lock the lid in place and ensure that the valve is in sealing position. Select Manual, High Pressure for 5 minutes.

5. When the timer beeps, do a natural pressure release. Carefully open the lid and fold in spinach and cook for a minute. Add the thick cashew cream for creamier soup and mix well
6. Add the black pepper and lemon juice. Season with salt and flavor. Serve with crackers, garlic rolls or garlic bread and enjoy!

Potato Corn Chowder

Preparation time: 25 minutes

Cook time: 5 minutes

Total time: 30 minutes

Servings: 6

Calories: 243kcal

Ingredients:

- 1 cup of diced onion
- 2 cloves garlic, minced
- 1 cup of diced carrots
- 1 cup of diced celery
- 6 cups of diced yellow or gold potatoes (about 6 medium potatoes)
- 1 bay leaf
- 1 tsp. of dried thyme
- 4 cups of vegetable broth
- 2 cups of frozen corn, defrosted
- ½ cup of raw cashews
- ½ cup of water
- Pinch of salt to taste
- Pepper to taste

Cooking Instructions:

1. Press the Sauté function on the Instant Pot and add the onion. Add a drop of water and sauté the onion for a few minutes until the onion is slightly soft.
2. Add the garlic and cook for additional 30 seconds. Add the carrots and celery. Sauté for additional few minutes until the vegetables begin to soften. Select the Cancel button.
3. Add the potatoes, bay leaf, thyme, and vegetable broth into the bottom of your Instant Pot. Give everything a good stir to combine. Close and lock the lid in place.
4. Select Manual, High Pressure for 4 minutes. In a blender, combine together the cashews and water and blend until smooth to make the cashew cream. When the timer beeps, do a quick pressure release.
5. Carefully open the lid and add the corn to the soup and stir. Pour in the cashew cream and give everything a good stir to combine. Season with salt and pepper, to taste, and serve immediately.

Mushroom Bourguignon

Preparation time: 15 minutes

Cook time: 5 hours

Total time: 10 hours 15 minutes

Servings: 2

Ingredients:

- 1 medium onion, chopped
- 3 large cloves of garlic, minced
- 2 carrots, cut into medium-sized sticks
- 5 cups of button mushrooms, cut into halves or quarters depending on their size
- 1 cup of red wine (vegan brand)
- 4 tbsp. of tomato paste
- 1 tsp. of dried marjoram
- 1 cup of vegetable broth
- 3 tsp. of dried Italian herbs (We used thyme, basil, rosemary, and oregano)
- 1 sprig fresh rosemary, chopped
- 1 tbsp. of corn starch + 2 tbsp. of water
- Pinch of salt, to taste
- Black pepper, to taste

Cooking Instructions:

1. Select the "Sauté" function on your Instant Pot and add some oil. Sauté the onions for about 3 minutes or until they become translucent.
2. Add the garlic, the mushrooms, and the carrots. Sauté for about 3 minutes. Add the tomato paste and sauté for additional 1 minute.
3. Deglaze the pot with red wine and vegetable broth to remove any browned bit stuck to the bottom of the pot. Add the herbs and season with salt and pepper to taste.
4. Close and lock the lid in place and ensure that the valve is in sealing position. Select Manual, High Pressure for 8 minutes. Whisk the cornstarch in a medium bowl with 2 tablespoons of water.
5. When the timer beeps, do a natural pressure release. Carefully open the lid and stir in the corn starch. Press the Sauté function and cook for about 3 minutes until the sauce becomes thicker.
6. Serve with fettuccine and enjoy!

Vegan Potato Curry

Preparation time: 10 minutes

Cook time: 40 minutes

Total time: 50 minutes

Servings: 5

Ingredients:

- 1 small yellow onion, chopped
- 4 large cloves of garlic, chopped finely
- 900g / about 5 heaping cups of baby potatoes
- 2 tbsp. of curry powder or curry paste
- 500mls / around 2 cups of water
- 400g / 2 heaping cups of fresh green beans, chopped into bite sized pieces
- 1 400ml can coconut milk, full fat or light
- 1 tbsp. of sugar, optional
- Pinch of salt
- Pepper to taste
- 1 tsp. of chili pepper flakes or a small fresh chili chopped, optional
- 3 tablespoons arrowroot powder, or corn starch

Cooking Instructions:

1. Press the Sauté button on your Instant Pot and add a few drops of water. Add the onion and sauté until translucent. Add the garlic and sauté for additional 1 minute.
2. Press the Cancel function. Add all the remaining ingredients into the bottom of your Instant Pot except for the green beans and arrowroot/cornstarch.
3. Close and lock the lid in place and ensure that the valve is in sealing position. Select Manual, High Pressure for 20 minutes. When the timer beeps, do a natural pressure release.
4. Press the Cancel button. Carefully open the lid and press the Sauté button. In a medium bowl, add the arrowroot/cornstarch and mix into it a few tablespoons of water.
5. Pour the mixture into the Instant Pot, stirring constantly. Season with salt and pepper to taste. Add the green beans and sauté for about 5 minutes until they are tender and the gravy has thickened.
6. Serve immediately and enjoy!

Vegan Lentil Chili

Preparation time: 10 minutes

Cook time: 19 minutes

Total time: 44 minutes

Servings: 6

Ingredients:

- 1 tbsp. of olive oil
- 1 onion, chopped
- 4 cloves minced garlic
- 2 carrots, chopped
- 1-2 jalapeños, chopped
- 1 ½ tbsp. chili powder
- 1 tbsp. of cumin
- ½ tsp. of ground coriander
- 1 tsp. of dried oregano
- ½ - ¾ tsp. of salt
- 1 (15 oz.) can crushed tomatoes
- 1 (28 oz.) can fire roasted diced tomatoes
- 2 cups of brown or green lentils (We used French green lentils)
- 4 cups of vegetable broth
- 1 tsp. of fresh lime juice
- ½ cup of chopped fresh cilantro

Cooking Instructions:

1. Select the Sauté function on your Instant Pot and add the olive oil.
2. Add the onion, garlic, carrots and jalapeños and cook until soft, about 3-4 minutes. Add the spices and rest of the ingredients except for lime juice and cilantro.
3. Close and lock the lid in place and ensure that the valve is in sealing position. Select Manual, High Pressure for 15 minutes.
4. When the timer beeps, do a quick pressure release. Carefully open the lid and stir in lime juice and cilantro.
5. Serve and enjoy!

Maple Bourbon Sweet Potato Chili

Preparation time: 10 minutes

Cook time 20 minutes

Total time 30 minutes

Servings: 4

Ingredients:

- 1 tablespoon of cooking oil
- 1 medium yellow onion, thinly sliced
- 2-3 cloves garlic, minced
- 4 cups of sweet potatoes, peeled and cubed into 1/2" pieces
- 2 cups of vegetable broth
- 1 ½ tablespoon of chili powder
- 2 teaspoons of cumin
- ½ teaspoon of paprika
- ¼ teaspoon of cayenne pepper
- 2 (15) oz. cans kidney beans, drained and rinsed
- 1 (15) oz. can diced tomatoes
- ¼ cup of bourbon
- 2 tablespoons of maple syrup
- Pinch of salt
- Pepper, to taste
- A few fresh springs of cilantro
- 2 green onions, diced
- 3 small corn tortillas, toasted and sliced (optional)

Cooking Instructions:

1. Press the Sauté button on your Instant Pot and add the oil.
2. When hot, add the onions and cook for about 5 minutes, stirring occasionally, until onions are translucent. Add the garlic and cook for additional 30 seconds.
3. Add the cubed sweet potatoes, chili powder, cumin, paprika, and cayenne pepper, stirring until vegetables are well coated. Add the vegetable broth, beans, tomatoes, maple syrup, and bourbon.
4. Close and lock the lid in place and ensure that the valve is in sealing position. Select Manual, High Pressure for 15 minutes.
5. When the timer beeps, do a quick pressure release. Carefully open the lid and check the potato for doneness. The potatoes should be tender.

6. If using tortillas, lightly oil a cast iron skillet and pan fry the tortillas on each side for about 2-3 minutes until crispy.
7. Remove from heat and allow to cool before cutting into thin strips. Serve with cilantro, green onions, and toasted tortillas.

Green Chile Stew

Preparation time: 30 minutes

Cook time: 38 minutes

Total time: 1 hour 8 minutes

Yield: 10 -12 bowls

Ingredients:

The Meat:

- ½ package of butler soy curls rehydrated
- 1 teaspoon of chili powder
- 1 teaspoon ground cumin
- 1 teaspoon of garlic powder
- 1 teaspoon of onion powder

The Broth:

- 1 medium yellow onion, diced
- 2 carrots, diced
- 2 stalks celery, diced
- 4-5 cloves garlic
- 2 cups of vegetable broth
- 2 cups of water
- 1 teaspoon of oregano
- 1 cup of dried rinsed, Pinto Beans

The Stew:

- 3 Yukon gold potatoes, cubed
- 15 ounces can fire roasted tomatoes
- 24 ounces package Select New Mexico Green Chiles
- ¼ cup of lime juice
- ¼ teaspoon of salt
- ¼ teaspoon of ground pepper

Cooking Instructions:

1. Press the Sauté button on your Instant Pot and saute your desired 'meat'.
2. Add the garlic powder, onion powder, chili powder, and cumin and stir occasionally until lightly browned for a couple of minutes.

3. Deglaze the with a little veggie broth to avoid sticking to the bottom of the pot. Transfer to a bowl and set aside.
4. Add the onion, carrots, and celery and sauté until soft and translucent. Add some veggie broth as required to avoid sticking. Scrape up any browned bits on bottom of pot.
5. Add the minced garlic and stir for 1 minute. Press the Cancel button. Add remaining veggie broth, water, oregano, and dried Beans.
6. Close and lock the lid in place and ensure that the valve is in sealing position. Select Manual, High Pressure for 30 minutes.
7. When the timer beeps, do a natural pressure release for about 10 minutes, then quick release any remaining pressure.
8. Carefully open the lid and stir broth and add potatoes, chilies, tomatoes, and the "meat" you reserved aside. Close and lock the lid in place.
9. Select Manual, High Pressure for 8 minutes. When the timer beeps, do a quick pressure release.
10. Carefully open the lid and stir in lime juice. Stir in masa flour - 1 tablespoon at time, until your desired thickness is achieved.
11. Serve and enjoy!

Vegetable Barley Soup

Preparation time: 10 minutes

Cook time: 30 minutes

Total time: 40 minutes

Ingredients:

- 2 garlic cloves, minced
- 1 small trimmed leek (7 oz. 1 cup), well-rinsed sliced
- 3 small carrots (6 oz. total, 1 ½ cups), sliced
- 3 stalks celery with leaves (6 oz. total, 2 cups), sliced
- 8 ounces mushrooms (3 cups), sliced
- 7 cups of water
- 2 cubes of vegetable bouillon
- 1 tbsp. of Italian seasoning
- ¼ tsp. of ground black pepper
- ½ cup of dried pearled barley

Cooking Instructions:

1. Add all the ingredients into the bottom of your Instant Pot and give everything a good stir.
2. Close and lock the lid in place and ensure that the valve is in sealing position. Select the "Soup" button to cook for 30 minutes.
3. When the timer beeps, do a quick pressure release. Carefully remove the lid and give everything a good stir.
4. Serve immediately and enjoy!

Vegan Butter Chicken

Preparation time: 10 minutes

Cook time: 35 minutes

Total time: 45 minutes

Servings: 3

Ingredients:

- 3 large ripe tomatoes or 1 15 ounces can diced tomatoes
- 4 cloves of garlic
- ½ inch cube of ginger
- 1 hot or mild green chili, We used serrano
- ¾ cup of water
- ½ - 1 teaspoon of garam masala
- ½ teaspoon of paprika or Kashmiri chili powder
- ¼ - ½ teaspoon of cayenne
- ¾ teaspoon of salt
- 1 cup of soy curls (dry, not rehydrated)
- 1 cup of cooked chickpeas
- Cashew cream made with ¼ cup of soaked cashews blended with ½ cup of water
- ½ teaspoon of garam masala
- ½ teaspoon of sugar or sweetener
- 1 teaspoon of kasoori methi - dried fenugreek leaves or add a ¼ teaspoon of ground mustard
- ½ moderately hot green chili, finely chopped, or 2 tablespoons of finely chopped green bell pepper
- ½ teaspoon of minced or finely chopped ginger
- ¼ cup of cilantro for garnish

Cooking Instructions:

1. Add the tomatoes, garlic, ginger, chili in your blender with water and blend everything until smooth.
2. Add the pureed tomato mixture into the bottom of your Instant Pot. Add the soy curls, chickpeas, spices and salt. Close and lock the lid in place and seal the vent.
3. Select Manual, High Pressure for 10 minutes. When the timer beeps, do a quick pressure release. Press the Sauté function.
4. Add the cashew cream, garam masala, sweetener and fenugreek leaves and give everything a good mix. Bring the pot to a boil, taste and adjust the seasoning with salt and sweetener.

5. Add more cayenne and salt if desired. Fold in the chopped green chili, ginger and cilantro. Select the Cancel function.
6. Add some vegan butter or oil for additional buttery flavor. Serve warm over rice or with flatbread or Naan and enjoy.

INSTANT POT APPETIZER RECIPES

Homemade Peaches and Cream Oatmeal

Preparation time: 15 minutes

Cook time: 10 minutes

Total time: 25 minutes

Servings: 8

Ingredients:

- 4 cups of Old Fashioned Oats
- 3 ½ cups of water
- 3 ½ cups of milk
- 1 tsp. of salt
- 1 tsp. of ground cinnamon
- 1/3 cup of sugar
- 4 peaches

Cooking Instructions:

1. Prepare the peaches by washing, peeling, and chopping and set a few slices aside for garnish.
2. Dump all the ingredients into the bottom of your Instant Pot and give everything a good stir. Close and lock the lid in place.
3. Select the Multigrain button for 6 minutes. When the timer beeps, do a natural pressure release.
4. Carefully open the lid and stir. Serve with sugar, brown sugar, milk, cream, and extra sliced peaches. Enjoy!

Cocktail Meatballs

Preparation time: 3 minutes

Cook time: 7 minutes

Total time: 10 minutes

Yield: 64 pieces

Ingredients:

- 2 lb. of Cooked Perfect Homestyle Meatballs
- ¼ cup of brown sugar
- ¼ cup of honey
- ½ cup of ketchup
- 2 tbsp. of soy sauce
- 1 tbsp. of minced garlic
- Garnish with sliced green onions (optional)

Cooking Instructions:

1. Add the brown sugar, honey, ketchup, soy sauce, and garlic into the bottom of your Instant Pot.
2. Press the Sauté function and stir to combine. When the pot comes to a boil, add the frozen cooked meatballs.
3. Close and lock the lid in place and ensure that the valve is in sealing position. Select Manual, High Pressure for 5 minutes.
4. When the timer beeps, do a natural pressure release. Carefully remove the lid and give everything a good stir.
5. Serve warm and enjoy!

Buffalo Ranch Chicken Dip

Preparation time: 2 minutes

Cook time: 15 minutes

Total time: 17 minutes

Servings: 6

Calories: 526 kcal

Ingredients:

- 1 lb. of chicken breast
- 1 packet ranch dip
- 1 cup of Hot Sauce
- 1 stick butter
- 16 ounces cheddar cheese
- 8 ounces cream cheese

Cooking Instructions:

1. Add the chicken, cream cheese, butter, hot sauce, and a packet of ranch dip into the bottom of your Instant Pot.
2. Close and lock the lid in place and ensure that the valve is in sealing position.
3. Select Manual, High Pressure for 15 minutes. When the timer beeps, do a quick pressure release.
4. Carefully remove the lid and shred the chicken with two forks. Stir in cheddar cheese.
5. Serve with chips and enjoy!

Beer-Braised Pulled Ham

Preparation time: 10 minutes

Cook time: 20 minutes

Total time: 30 minutes

Servings: 16

Ingredients:

- 2 bottles (12 oz. each) beer or nonalcoholic beer
- ¾ cup of German or Dijon mustard, divided
- ½ tsp. of coarsely ground pepper
- 1 fully cooked bone-in ham (4 lb.)
- 4 fresh rosemary sprigs
- 16 pretzel hamburger buns, split
- Dill pickle slices, optional

Cooking Instructions:

1. Whisk together the beer, ½ cup of mustard and pepper into the bottom of your Instant Pot. Add the ham and rosemary.
2. Close and lock the lid in place and ensure that the valve is in sealing position. Select Manual, High Pressure for 20 minutes.
3. When the timer beeps, do a natural pressure release for about 10 minutes, then quick release any remaining pressure.
4. Carefully open the lid and discard the rosemary sprigs. Remove the ham and drain fat from liquid remaining in the pot.
5. Press the Sauté button and adjust for high heat. Bring the pot to a boil for about 5 minutes. Shred the meat with two forks. Discard bone.
6. Add the meat back into the pot, heat through and give everything a good stir. Add the shredded ham on pretzel bun bottoms on a serving bowl with remaining mustard and, if desired, dill pickle slices.

Cranberry Pecan Brie

Preparation time: 10 minutes

Cook time: 15 minutes

Total time: 25 minutes

Ingredients:

- 1 (8 oz.) round of Brie
- ¼ cup of cranberry jalapeno preserves
- 3 tbsp. of candied pecans
- 1 tsp. of minced fresh thyme

Cooking Instructions:

1. Prepare the brie by slicing through the rind on top of the Brie in a grid pattern. Add the brie in a 7" spring form pan that will fit into your Instant Pot.
2. Cover the spring form tightly with foil. Pour 1 cup of water into the bottom of your Instant Pot and place the trivet.
3. Carefully place the spring form pan trivet. Close and lock the lid in place and ensure that the valve is in sealing position.
4. Select Manual, High Pressure for 15 minutes. When the timer beeps, do a quick pressure release. Carefully open the lid and check to make sure cheese is melted.
5. Flip over to a serving bowl and top with preserves, pecans and thyme. Serve warm with baguette slices, crostini, pita wedges, or crackers for dipping.

Prosciutto-wrapped Asparagus Canes

Preparation time: 5 minutes

Cook time: 7 minutes

Total time: 12 minutes

Ingredients:

- 1 pound (500g) thick Asparagus
- 8 ounces (225g) thinly sliced Prosciutto

Cooking Instructions:

1. Pour 1 to 2 cups of water into the bottom of your Instant Pot. Wrap the asparagus spears in prosciutto.
2. Lay any extra un-wrapped spears in a single layer along trivet. Arrange the prosciutto-wrapped asparagus on top in a single layer on top of the trivet.
3. Place the trivet into the Instant Pot. Close and lock the lid in place and ensure that the valve is in sealing position.
4. Select Manual, High Pressure for 7 minutes. When the timer beeps, do a natural pressure release.
5. Carefully open the lid and remove the steamer basket. Add the asparagus on a serving bowl to avoid cooking by residual heat from Instant Pot.
6. Serve warm and enjoy!

Barbecue Kielbasa Bites

Preparation time: 5 minutes

Cook time: 10 minutes

Total time: 15 minutes

Serves 4-5

Ingredients:

- 1 pound of Kielbasa
- Homemade Barbecue Sauce
- ½ cup of water

Cooking Instructions:

1. Place the sausage on a cutting board and slice into rounds, about ½ inch - ¾ inch thick. Add the sliced sausage in a medium bowl and set aside.
2. Pour the homemade sweet and tangy barbecue sauce into the bottom of your Instant Pot and along with ½ cup of water.
3. Add the reserved kielbasa and give everything a good stir. Close and lock the lid in place and ensure that the valve is in sealing position.
4. Select Manual, High Pressure for 5 minutes. When the timer beeps, do a natural pressure release. Carefully open the lid and allow the sausage to thicken as it cools.
5. Serve and cnjoy!

Apple Pie Steel Cut Oats

Preparation time: 5 minutes

Cook time: 20 minutes

Total time: 25 minutes

Servings: 6

Calories: 120 kcal

Ingredients:

- 1 cup of steel cut oats
- 1-2 apples, diced
- 1 ½ teaspoon of cinnamon
- ½ teaspoon of salt
- ¼ teaspoon of nutmeg fresh grated
- 3 cups of water

Cooking Instructions:

1. Add all the ingredients into the bottom of your Instant Pot.
2. Close and lock the lid in place and ensure that the valve is in sealing position. Select Manual, High Pressure for 5 minutes.
3. When the timer beeps, do a natural pressure release for about 10 minutes, then quick release any remaining pressure. Carefully open the lid and give everything a good stir.
4. Serve with your desired toppings like a few pecans, a little almond milk, and a drizzle of maple syrup for sweetening.

Cheddar Bacon Ale Dip

Preparation time: 15 minutes

Cook time: 10 minutes

Total time: 25 minutes

Servings: 4 ½ cups

Ingredients:

- 18 oz. cream cheese, softened
- ¼ cup of sour cream
- 1 - ½ tbsp. of Dijon mustard
- 1 tsp. of garlic powder
- 1 cup of beer or nonalcoholic beer
- 1 lb. of bacon strips, cooked and crumbled
- 2 cups of shredded cheddar cheese
- ¼ cup of heavy whipping cream
- 1 green onion, thinly sliced
- Soft pretzel bites

Cooking Instructions:

1. In a medium bowl, combine together the cream cheese, sour cream, and mustard and garlic powder until smooth.
2. Pour the mixture into the bottom of your Instant Pot. Stir in beer; add the bacon, and set 2 tbsp. aside. Close and lock the lid in place.
3. Select Manual, High Pressure for 5 minutes. When the timer beeps, do a quick pressure release. Carefully open the lid and stir in cheese and heavy cream.
4. Press the Sauté button, and adjust for normal heat. Cook and stir for about 3 minutes or until mixture has thickened.
5. Transfer to serving bowl and sprinkle with onion and reserved bacon. Serve with pretzel bun bites and enjoy!

Hoisin Meatballs

Preparation time: 20 minutes

Cook time: 10 minutes

Total time: 30 minutes

Yield: about 2 dozen

Ingredients:

- 1 cup of dry red wine or beef broth
- 3 tbsp. of hoisin sauce
- 2 tbsp. of soy sauce
- 1 large egg, lightly beaten
- 4 green onions, chopped
- ¼ cup of finely chopped onion
- ¼ cup of minced fresh cilantro
- 2 garlic cloves, minced
- ½ tsp. of salt
- ½ tsp. of pepper
- 1 lb. of ground beef
- 1 lb. of ground pork
- Sesame seeds

Cooking Instructions:

1. Add the together wine, hoisin sauce and soy sauce and whisk everything. Press the Sauté function and bring the pot to a boil.
2. In a medium bowl, combine together the nest seven ingredients. Mix the beef and pork and shape into 1-1/2-in. meatballs.
3. Add the mixture into the bottom of your Instant Pot. Close and lock the lid in place and ensure that the valve is in sealing position.
4. Select Manual, High Pressure for 10 minutes. When the timer beeps, do a quick pressure release. Carefully open the lid and sprinkle with sesame seeds.
5. Serve and enjoy!

INSTANT POT DESSERT RECIPES

Blueberry Cornmeal Breakfast Cake

Preparation time: 10 minutes

Cook time: 45 minutes

Total time: 45 minutes

Servings: 4

Ingredients:

- 1 8.5 ounces box Jiffy cornbread mix
- 2 tbsp. of ground flax seed
- 2 tbsp. of chia seeds
- 1 egg
- ½ cup of milk
- 1 cup of blueberries
- 2 tbsp. of honey

Cooking Instructions:

1. Pour 1 cup of water into the bottom of your Instant Pot and place the trivet. Generously grease a spring form pan that will fit inside your Instant Pot.
2. In a medium bowl, whisk together the cornbread mix, flax, chia, egg, and milk then gently stir in blueberries.
3. Add the batter into the spring form pan and place the pan on top of the trivet. Close and lock the lid in place and ensure that the valve is in sealing position.
4. Select Manual, High Pressure for 35 minutes. When the timer beeps, do a natural pressure release for about 5 minutes, then quick release any remaining pressure.
5. Carefully open the lid and drizzle with honey, slice into wedges, and serve!

Apple Bread with Salted Caramel Icing

Preparation time: 10 minutes

Cook time: 1 hour 10 minutes

Total time: 1 hour 10 minutes

Yield: 10

Calories: 551 kcal

Ingredients:

- 3 cups of apples Peeled Cored, and cubed
- 1 cup of sugar
- 2 eggs
- 1 tablespoon of vanilla
- 1 tablespoon of apple pie spice
- 2 cups of flour
- 1 stick butter
- 1 tablespoon of baking powder

For the Topping:

- 1 stick salted butter
- 2 cups of brown sugar
- 1 cup of heavy cream
- 2 cups of powdered sugar

Cooking Instructions:

1. In a medium bowl, cream together the eggs, butter, apple pie spice, and sugar until creamy and smooth. Stir in your apples.
2. In a separate bowl, mix together the flour and baking powder. Add the flour mix to the wet mix. The batter should be thick. Pour the mixture into your 7" spring form pan.
3. Pour 1 cup of water into the bottom of your Instant Pot and place the trivet. Place the spring form pan on top the trivet. Close and lock the lid in place.
4. Select Manual, High Pressure for 70 minutes. When the timer beeps, do a quick pressure release. Carefully open the lid and allow to cool.
5. Serve topped with Icing.

Chunky Apple Cake

Preparation time: 5 minutes

Cook time: 55 minutes

Total time: 60 minutes

Servings: 4-6

Ingredients:

- ¾ cup of vanilla Greek yogurt
- ½ cup of vegetable oil
- 1 cup of sugar
- 1 egg
- 1 tsp. of vanilla
- 2 cups of peeled & chopped apples
- 2 cups of all-purpose flour
- ½ cup of oatmeal
- 1 tsp. of baking soda
- ½ tsp. of kosher salt
- ½ tsp. of grated nutmeg
- 1 tsp. of cinnamon
- ¼ cup of chopped walnuts or pecans
- ¼ cup of shredded sweetened coconut

Cooking Instructions:

1. Grease a spring form pan that will fit into Instant Pot. In a medium bowl, whisk together the yogurt, oil, sugar, egg, vanilla, and chopped apples.
2. Stir in flour, oatmeal, baking soda, salt, nutmeg, and cinnamon until just combined, and do not overmix. Fold in nuts and coconut then pour batter into the spring form pan.
3. Pour 1 ½ cups of water into the bottom of your Instant Pot and place the trivet. Place the spring form pan on top the trivet.
4. Close and lock the lid in place and ensure that the valve is in sealing position. Select Manual, High Pressure for 30 minutes.
5. When the timer beeps, do a natural pressure release for about 10 minutes, then quick release any remaining pressure. Carefully open the lid and remove the pan.
6. Loosen the edges with knife, and flip on a serving bowl.
7. Serve and enjoy!

Apple Crisp

Servings: 3-4

Preparation time: 5 minutes

Cook time: 8 minutes

Total time: 13 minutes

Ingredients:

- 5 medium sized apples, peeled and chopped into chunks
- 2 teaspoons of cinnamon
- ½ teaspoon of nutmeg
- ½ cup of water
- 1 tablespoon of maple syrup
- 4 tablespoons of butter
- ¾ cup of old fashioned rolled oats
- ¼ cup of flour
- ¼ cup of brown sugar
- ½ teaspoon of salt

Cooking Instructions:

1. Add the apples into the bottom of your Instant Pot. Sprinkle with cinnamon and nutmeg.
2. Pour the water and maple syrup. Melt the butter. In a medium bowl, mix together the melted butter, oats, flour, brown sugar and salt.
3. Drop the mixture by spoonful on top of the apples. Close and lock the lid in place and ensure that the valve is in sealing position.
4. Select Manual, High Pressure for 8 minutes. When the timer beeps, do a natural pressure release for about 15 minutes.
5. Carefully open the lid and allow the sauce to cool and thicken for a couple of minutes.
6. Serve warm and top with vanilla ice cream if desired.

Molten Mocha Cake

Preparation time: 10 minutes

Cook time: 25 minutes

Total time: 35 minutes

Servings: 6

Ingredients:

- 1 cup of water
- 4 large Nellie's Free Range Eggs
- 1 - ½ cups of sugar
- ½ cup of butter, melted
- 1 tbsp. of vanilla extract
- 1 cup of all-purpose flour
- ½ cup of baking cocoa
- 1 tbsp. of instant coffee granules
- ¼ tsp. of salt
- Fresh raspberries or sliced fresh strawberries and vanilla ice cream, optional

Cooking Instructions:

1. Add the water into the bottom of your Instant Pot. In a medium bowl, beat the eggs, sugar, butter and vanilla until blended.
2. In a separate bowl, whisk together flour, cocoa, coffee granules and salt; gently beat into egg mixture. Add the mixture spring form pan that will fit into your Instant Pot.
3. Slightly cover the pan with foil. Place the spring form pan on the trivet and place into the pot. Close and lock the lid in place and ensure that the valve is in sealing position.
4. Select Manual, High Pressure for 25 minutes. When the timer beeps, do a natural pressure release for about 10 minutes, then quick release any remaining pressure.
5. Carefully open the lid and check for doneness with a toothpick. The toothpick should come out with moist crumbs.
6. Serve warm cake with berries and ice cream and enjoy!

Mason Jar Steel Cut Oats

Preparation time: 5 minutes

Cook time: 20 minutes

Total time: 25 minutes

Serves: 1

Ingredients:

- ¼ cup of steel cut oats
- 2 tbsp. of pure maple syrup
- 1-2 tsp. of chia seeds
- Pinch of salt
- ½ cup of the extras (fresh or dried fruit, nuts, coconut, spices, etc)
- 1 cup hot or room temperature tap water

Cooking Instructions:

1. Add together the oats, syrup, chia seeds, salt and the extras into a pint size mason jar. Pour the water, leaving 1½ inches of headspace.
2. Give everything a good stir until everything is well distributed and the chia seeds aren't clumping together. Pour 1 cup of water into the bottom of your Instant Pot and place the trivet.
3. Select Manual, High Pressure for 20 minutes. When the timer beeps, do a natural pressure release for about 10 minutes, then quick release any remaining pressure.
4. Carefully open the lid and remove the jars. Do not open the jars until contents have cooled. Give the oats a good stir and top with a dollop of frozen whipped cream and garnish.
5. Serve and enjoy!

Applesauce

Preparation time: 2 minutes

Cook time: 8 minutes

Total time 10 minutes

Servings: 4

Calories: 143 kcal

Ingredients:

- 6-8 medium to large apples Granny Smith, Gala, McIntosh, Fuji, etc.
- 1 cup of water
- 1-2 drops of cinnamon essential oil
- 1 teaspoon of organic cinnamon. optional

Cooking Instructions:

1. Use a knife to cut the apples into 2-inch chunks. Discard the core, stem and seeds.
2. Add the apples into the bottom of your Instant Pot along with 1 cup of water. Close and lock the lid in place and ensure that the valve is in sealing position.
3. Select Manual, High Pressure for 8 minutes. When the timer beeps, do a quick pressure release. Carefully remove the lid and drain any excess water.
4. Use an electric mixer or immersion blender to blend the apple until your desired consistency is achieved.
5. Add 1-2 drops of cinnamon oil or cinnamon powder to taste. Serve and enjoy!